LONDON'S ESSAYS OF REVOLT

Jack London, 1902
in England doing
research on the
"The People of The
Abyss"

London's Essays of Revolt

JACK LONDON

Edited and Introduction by
LEONARD D. ABBOTT

ESSAYS OF REVOLT

JACK LONDON

Published by Frederick Ellis
6015 S. Virginia, Suite E365
Reno, Nevada
89502

ISBN 1-934568-554

CONTENTS

LONDON'S ESSAYS OF REVOLT

LONDON'S ESSAYS OF REVOLT

FOREWORD

JACK LONDON is one of the glories of our literature. For America he means something of what Maxim Gorky has meant for Russia. He emerged "out of the depths" in California thirty years ago to become a champion of romance and adventure and a Socialist crusader. He wrote no less than forty-eight books in sixteen years. When he died in 1916, at the age of forty, his name was carried to the ends of the earth; and ten years later his books are still being circulated by the thousand and his name is a household word.

All literature, in a sense, is autobiography; but seldom has a writer lived whose books so completely expressed his life and his changing moods as Jack London's did. His major experiences, beginning with his boyish exploits on the Oakland and San Francisco waterfronts, his march East with "Coxey's army," his trip to the Klondike region of Alaska, his exploration of the London slums, and including, subsequently, his cruise across the Pacific in a fifty-foot ketch, his work as a war-correspondent in Mexico and Japan, and his visits to Hawaii, are all vividly reflected in his writings.

The very titles of his books and stories show a kind of genius. What could be more fitting than *The White Silence*, *The Sea Wolf* or *The People of the Abyss*? The best-known and best-written of his tales is his dog-story, *The Call of the Wild*, but the story in which he is most intimately revealed is *Martin Eden*. This novel tells how a working boy rises from poverty, wrestles with life, with sex, and with social

3

and philosophic problems, only, in the end, to fall back baffled. *Martin Eden* has been wrongly interpreted as a glorification of the red-blooded "superman," trampling all things under foot. It is actually, as its author wrote to Upton Sinclair, "an attack on individualism."

To read the fifty-odd books of Jack London is a mental adventure of the most bracing sort. He wrote too much, and, in the end, he wrote, as he himself confessed, for money. Yet almost everything that he wrote is worth reading, and at his best he is unsurpassed.

The motive of all is *escape* from the commonplace routine to which most men and women are condemned in present-day society. In Jack London was the restlessness not only of his own blood, but also of the pioneers who had preceded him and made possible the settlement of the Pacific Coast. To them it had seemed a last frontier, but for him there could never be any "last"—his impulse was always to push forward, to extend boundaries, to open up new worlds to the human spirit.

Oyster pirates, skippers, sailors, hunters, gold-seekers, hoboes, explorers, half-breeds, trappers, Indian women, revolutionaries, prize-fighters and Nietzschean individualists troop across his pages. He was fascinated by primitive motives, and his formula has been summed up in the sentence: At bottom every man is a brute. And yet, by that law of opposites which works out so dramatically in human character, there was a gentle and kindly side to his nature, as those who knew him best have testified. He started as a philosophical materialist, a disciple of Haeckel. Before he died he became intensely interested in psychoanalysis.

A terrific "conflict" (in the psychoanalytic sense) raged in his soul throughout his life. His instinctive impulses were at war with those which civilization was breeding in him, and he never succeeded in completely reconciling the two. He was able, however, to gratify his lust for adventure in his trips to tropical islands and in long voyages. He enjoyed, if only for a time, his life as a ranchman in the "valley of the moon" in California. And he found enduring inspiration in his Socialist faith.

His first activities as a propagandist were in the ranks of the Socialist Labor Party. Later he joined the Socialist Party. He always prided himself on being a workingman, and, during the course of an address at a Socialist meeting in Los Angeles in 1905, he repudiated the chairman's characterization of him as "a ripe scholar, a profound philosopher, a literary genius and the foremost man of letters in America," and said: "Before people had given me any of these titles with which the chairman so lavishly credits me, I was working in a cannery, a pickle factory, was a sailor before the mast, and spent months at a time looking for work in the ranks of the unemployed; and it is the proletarian side of my life that I revere the most, and to which I will cling as long as I live." In the same year he carried to students in Eastern and Western universities the militant message: "The revolution is here now. Stop it who can!" He resigned from the Socialist Party a few months before his death "because of its lack of fire and fight, and its loss of emphasis on the class struggle."

The essays, confession, and story reprinted in this book belong to the youthful period of Jack London's Socialistic activities. We may find, in the sketch he has called *The Apostate*, the veritable picture of his own revolt, as an adolescent boy, against capitalism. In *The Dream of Debs* is prefigured a social rebellion not so very different from what the recent English "general strike" might easily have become. Not always an idealist, we find London in *The Scab* analyzing and evaluating the labor movement, measuring its possibilities by idealistic standards but telling truths with critical insight. The positive side of Jack London's social creed is embodied in his autobiographical essay, *What Life Means to Me*. This penetrates to the source of his power, the secret of his genius. Jack London, the propagandist, the man whose vision kindled the fire of youth throughout the country, is seen in all his strength and vigor in the essay *Revolution*. In this speech, delivered before the student bodies of universities from Yale to California, Jack London put all his power of persuasion of intelligent youth. To him Revolution was not an abstraction, not a far distant ideal, but a thing to be built purposely and lived in.

In his best moments he looked forward to a time when every man shall be a workingman, when parasitism shall be abolished, and when every influence shall invite us to the realization of our noblest visions.

LEONARD D. ABBOTT

New York City,
June, 1926.

THE APOSTATE

THE APOSTATE

Now I wake me up to work;
I pray the Lord I may not shirk.
If I should die before the night,
I pray the Lord my work's all right.
                              Amen.

"IF YOU don't git up, Johnny, I won't give you a bite to eat!"

The threat had no effect on the boy. He clung stubbornly
to sleep, fighting for its oblivion as the dreamer fights for
his dream. The boy's hands loosely clenched themselves, and
he made feeble, spasmodic blows at the air. These blows were
intended for his mother, but she betrayed practised familiarity
in avoiding them as she shook him roughly by the shoulder.

"Lemme 'lone!"

It was a cry that began, muffled, in the deeps of sleep,
that swiftly rushed upward, like a wail, into passionate bel-
ligerence, and that died away and sank down into an inarticu-
late whine. It was a bestial cry, as of a soul in torment,
filled with infinite protest and pain.

But she did not mind. She was a sad-eyed, tired-faced
woman, and she had grown used to this task, which she
repeated every day of her life. She got a grip on the bed-
clothes and tried to strip them down; but the boy, ceasing
his punching, clung to them desperately. In a huddle, at the
foot of the bed, he still remained covered. Then she tried
dragging the bedding to the floor. The boy opposed her. She
braced herself. Hers was the superior weight, and the boy
and bedding gave, the former instinctively following the latter in order to shelter against the chill of the room that bit
into his body.

As he toppled on the edge of the bed it seemed that he
must fall head-first to the floor. But consciousness fluttered

up in him. He righted himself and for a moment perilously balanced. Then he struck the floor on his feet. On the instant his mother seized him by the shoulders and shook him. Again his fists struck out, this time with more force and directness. At the same time his eyes opened. She released him. He was awake.

"All right," he mumbled.

She caught up the lamp and hurried out, leaving him in darkness.

"You'll be docked," she warned back at him.

He did not mind the darkness. When he had got into his clothes, he went out into the kitchen. His tread was very heavy for so thin and light a boy. His legs dragged with their own weight, which seemed unreasonable because they were such skinny legs. He drew a broken-bottomed chair to the table.

"Johnny!" his mother called sharply.

He arose as sharply from the chair, and, without a word went to the sink. It was a greasy, filthy sink. A smell came up from the outlet. He took no notice of it. That a sink should smell was to him part of the natural order, just as it was a part of the natural order that the soap should be grimy with dishwater and hard to lather. Nor did he try very hard to make it lather. Several splashes of the cold water from the running faucet completed the function. He did not wash his teeth. For that matter he had never seen a tooth-brush, nor did he know that there existed human beings in the world who were guilty of so great a foolishness as tooth washing.

"You might wash yourself wunst a day without bein' told," his mother complained.

She was holding a broken lid on the pot as she poured two cups of coffee. He made no remark, for this was a standing quarrel between them, and the one thing upon which his mother was hard as adamant. "Wunst" a day it was compulsory that he should wash his face. He dried himself on a greasy towel, damp and dirty and ragged, that left his face covered with shreds of lint.

"I wish we didn't live so far away," she said, as he sat down. "I try to do the best I can. You know that. But a dollar on the rent is such a savin', an' we've more room here. You know that."

He scarcely followed her. He had heard it all before, many times. The range of her thought was limited, and she was ever harking back to the hardship worked upon them by living so far from the mills.

"A dollar means more grub," he remarked sententiously. "I'd sooner do the walkin' and git the grub."

He ate hurriedly, half chewing the bread and washing the unmasticated chunks down with coffee. The hot and muddy liquid went by the name of coffee. Johnny thought it was coffee—and excellent coffee. That was one of the few of life's illusions that remained to him. He had never drunk real coffee in his life.

In addition to the bread, there was a small piece of cold pork. His mother refilled his cup with coffee. As he was finishing the bread, he began to watch if more was forthcoming. She intercepted his questioning glance.

"Now, don't be hoggish, Johnny," was her comment. "You've had your share. Your brothers an' sisters are smaller'n you."

He did not answer the rebuke. He was not much of a talker. Also, he ceased his hungry glancing for more. He was uncomplaining, with a patience that was as terrible as the school in which it had been learned. He finished his coffee, wiped his mouth on the back of his hand, and started to rise.

"Wait a second," she said hastily. "I guess the loaf can stand another slice—a thin un."

There was legerdemain in her actions. With all the seeming of cutting a slice from the loaf for him, she put loaf and slice back in the bread box and conveyed to him one of her own two slices. She believed she had deceived him, but he had noted her sleight-of-hand. Nevertheless, he took the bread shamelessly. He had a philosophy that his mother, what of her chronic sickliness, was not much of an eater anyway.

She saw that he was chewing the bread dry, and reached over and emptied her coffee cup into his.

"Don't set good somehow on my stomach this morning," she explained.

A distant whistle, prolonged and shrieking, brought both of them to their feet. She glanced at the tin alarm-clock on the shelf. The hands stood at half-past five. The rest of the factory world was just arousing from sleep. She drew a shawl about her shoulders, and on her head put a dingy hat, shapeless and ancient.

"We've got to run," she said, turning the wick of the lamp and blowing down the chimney.

They groped their way out and down the stairs. It was clear and cold, and Johnny shivered at the first contact with the outside air. The stars had not yet begun to pale in the sky, and the city lay in blackness. Both Johnny and his mother shuffled their feet as they walked. There was no ambition in the leg muscles to swing the feet clear of the ground.

After fifteen silent minutes, his mother turned off to the right.

"Don't be late," was her final warning from out of the dark that was swallowing her up.

He made no response, steadily keeping on his way. In the factory quarter, doors were opening everywhere, and he was soon one of a multitude that pressed onward through the dark. As he entered the factory gate the whistle blew again. He glanced at the east. Across a ragged sky-line of house-tops a pale light was beginning to creep. This much he saw of the day as he turned his back upon it and joined his work-gang.

He took his place in one of many long rows of machines. Before him, above a bin filled with small bobbins, were large bobbins revolving rapidly. Upon these he wound the jute-twine of the small bobbins. The work was simple. All that

was required was celerity. The small bobbins were emptied
so rapidly, and there were so many large bobbins that did the
emptying, that there were no idle moments.

He worked mechanically. When a small bobbin ran out,
he used his left hand for a brake, stopping the large bobbin
and at the same time, with thumb and forefinger, catching
the flying end of twine. Also, at the same time, with his
right hand, he caught up the loose twine-end of a small bobbin. These various acts with both hands were performed
simultaneously and swiftly. Then there would come a flash
of his hands as he looped the weaver's knot and released the
bobbin. There was nothing difficult about the weaver's
knots. He once boasted he could tie them in his sleep. And
for that matter, he sometimes did, toiling centuries long in
a single night at tying an endless succession of weaver's knots.

Some of the boys shirked, wasting time and machinery by
not replacing the small bobbins when they ran out. And
there was an overseer to prevent this. He caught Johnny's
neighbor at the trick, and boxed his ears.

"Look at Johnny there—why ain't you like him?" the
overseer wrathfully demanded.

Johnny's bobbins were running full blast, but he did not
thrill at the indirect praise. There had been a time . . .
but that was long ago, very long ago. His apathetic face
was expressionless as he listened to himself being held up as
a shining example. He was the perfect worker. He knew
that. He had been told so, often. It was a commonplace,
and besides it didn't seem to mean anything to him any more.
From the perfect worker he had evolved into the perfect
machine. When his work went wrong, it was with him as
with the machine, due to faulty material. It would have
been as possible for a perfect nail-die to cut imperfect nails
as for him to make a mistake.

And small wonder. There had never been a time when he
had not been in intimate relationship with machines. Machinery had almost been bred into him, and at any rate he
had been brought up on it. Twelve years before, there had

been a small flutter of excitement in the loom room of this very mill. Johnny's mother had fainted. They stretched her out on the floor in the midst of the shrieking machines. A couple of elderly women were called from their looms. The foreman assisted. And in a few minutes there was one more soul in the loom room than had entered by the doors. It was Johnny, born with the pounding, crashing roar of the looms in his ears, drawing with his first breath the warm, moist air that was thick with flying lint. He had coughed that first day in order to rid his lungs of the lint; and for the same reason he had coughed ever since.

The boy alongside of Johnny whimpered and sniffed. The boy's face was convulsed with hatred for the overseer who kept a threatening eye on him from a distance; but every bobbin was running full. The boy yelled terrible oaths into the whirling bobbins before him; but the sound did not carry half a dozen feet, the roaring of the room holding it in and containing it like a wall.

Of all this Johnny took no notice. He had a way of accepting things. Besides, things grow monotonous by repetition, and this particular happening he had witnessed many times. It seemed to him as useless to oppose the overseer as to defy the will of a machine. Machines were made to go in certain ways and to perform certain tasks. It was the same with the overseer.

But at eleven o'clock there was excitement in the room. In an apparently occult way the excitement instantly permeated everywhere. The one-legged boy who worked on the other side of Johnny bobbed swiftly across the floor to a bin truck that stood empty. Into this he dived out of sight, crutch and all. The superintendent of the mill was coming along, accompanied by a young man. He was well dressed and wore a starched shirt—a gentleman, in Johnny's classification of men, and also, "the Inspector."

He looked sharp at the boys as he passed along. When he did so, he was compelled to shout at the top of his lungs, at which moments his face was ludicrously contorted with the strain of making himself heard. His quick eye noted the empty machine alongside of Johnny's, but he said nothing. Johnny also caught his eye, and he stopped abruptly. He caught Johnny by the arm to draw him back a step from the machine; but with an exclamation of surprise he released the arm.

"Pretty skinny," the superintendent laughed anxiously.

"Pipe stems," was the answer. "Look at those legs. The boy's got the rickets—incipient, but he's got them. If epilepsy doesn't get him in the end, it will be because tuberculosis gets him first."

Johnny listened, but did not understand. Furthermore he was not interested in future ills. There was an immediate and more serious ill that threatened him in the form of the inspector.

"Now, my boy, I want you to tell me the truth," the inspector said, or shouted, bending close to the boy's ear to make him hear. "How old are you?"

"Fourteen," Johnny lied, and he lied with the full force of his lungs. So loudly did he lie that it started him off in a dry, hacking cough that lifted the lint which had been settling in his lungs all morning.

"Looks sixteen at least," said the superintendent.

"Or sixty," snapped the inspector.

"He's always looked that way."

"How long?" asked the inspector quickly.

"For years. Never gets a bit older."

"Or younger, I dare say. I suppose he's worked here all those years?"

"Off and on—but that was before the new law was passed," the superintendent hastened to add.

"Machine idle?" the inspector asked, pointing at the unoccupied machine beside Johnny's, in which the part filled bobbins were flying like mad.

"Looks that way." The superintendent motioned the overseer to him and shouted in his ear and pointed at the machine. "Machine's idle," he reported back to the inspector.

They passed on, and Johnny returned to his work, relieved in that the ill had been averted. But the one-legged boy was not so fortunate. The sharp-eyed inspector hauled him out at arm's length from the bin truck. His lips were quivering, and his face had all the expression of one upon whom was fallen profound and irremediable disaster. The overseer looked astounded, as though for the first time he had laid eyes on the boy, while the superintendent's face expressed shock and displeasure.

"I know him," the inspector said. "He's twelve years old. I've had him discharged from three factories inside the year. This makes the fourth."

He turned to the one-legged boy. "You promised me, word and honor, that you'd go to school."

The one-legged boy burst into tears. "Please, Mr. Inspector, two babies died on us, and we're awful poor."

"What makes you cough that way?" the inspector demanded, as though charging him with crime.

And as in denial of guilt, the one-legged boy replied: "It ain't nothin'. I jes' caught a cold last week, Mr. Inspector, that's all."

In the end the one-legged boy went out of the room with the inspector, the latter accompanied by the anxious and protesting superintendent. After that monotony settled down again. The long morning and the longer afternoon wore away and the whistle blew for quitting time. Darkness had already fallen when Johnny passed out through the factory gate. In the interval the sun had made a golden ladder of the sky, flooded the world with its gracious warmth, and dropped down and disappeared in the west behind a ragged sky-line of housetops.

Supper was the family meal of the day—the one meal at which Johnny encountered his younger brothers and sisters. It partook of the nature of an encounter, to him, for he was very old, while they were distressingly young. He had no patience with their excessive and amazing juvenility. He did not understand it. His own childhood was too far behind him. He was like an old and irritable man, annoyed by the turbulence of their young spirits that was to him arrant silliness. He glowered silently over his food, finding compensation in the thought that they would soon have to go to work. That would take the edge off of them and make them sedate and dignified—like him. Thus it was, after the fashion of the human, that Johnny made of himself a yardstick with which to measure the universe.

During the meal, his mother explained in various ways and with infinite repetition that she was trying to do the best she could; so that it was with relief, the scant meal ended, that Johnny shoved back his chair and arose. He debated for a moment between bed and the front door, and finally went out the latter. He did not go far. He sat down on the stoop, his knees drawn up and his narrow shoulders drooping forward, his elbows on his knees and the palms of his hands supporting his chin.

As he sat there, he did no thinking. He was just resting. So far as his mind was concerned, it was asleep. His brothers and sisters came out, and with other children played noisily about him. An electric globe on the corner lighted their frolics. He was peevish and irritable, that they knew; but the spirit of adventure lured them into teasing him. They joined hands before him, and, keeping time with their bodies, chanted in his face weird and uncomplimentary doggerel. At first he snarled curses at them—curses he had learned from the lips of various foremen. Finding this futile, and remembering his dignity, he relapsed into dogged silence.

His brother Will, next to him in age, having just passed his tenth birthday, was the ringleader. Johnny did not possess particularly kindly feelings toward him. His life had early been imbittered by continual giving over and giving way to Will. He had a definite feeling that Will was greatly in his debt and was ungrateful about it. In his own playtime, far back in the dim past, he had been robbed of a large part of that playtime by being compelled to take care of Will. Will was a baby then, and then, as now, their mother had

spent her days in the mills. To Johnny had fallen the part
of little father and little mother as well.

Will seemed to show the benefit of the giving over and the
giving way. He was well-built, fairly rugged, as tall as his
elder brother and even heavier. It was as though the life-
blood of the one had been diverted into the other's veins.
And in spirits it was the same. Johnny was jaded, worn out,
without resilience, while his younger brother seemed bursting
and spilling over with exuberance.

The mocking chant rose louder and louder. Will leaned
closer as he danced, thrusting out his tongue. Johnny's left
arm shot out and caught the other around the neck. At the
same time he rapped his bony fist to the other's nose. It was
a pathetically bony fist, but that it was sharp to hurt was
evidenced by the squeal of pain it produced. The other children were uttering frightened cries, while Johnny's sister,
Jennie, had dashed into the house.

He thrust Will from him, kicked him savagely on the
shins, then reached for him and slammed him face downward
in the dirt. Nor did he release him till the face had been
rubbed into the dirt several times. Then the mother arrived,
an anæmic whirlwind of solicitude and maternal wrath.

"Why can't he leave me alone?" was Johnny's reply to
her upbraiding. "Can't he see I'm tired?"

"I'm as big as you," Will raged in her arms, his face a
mess of tears, dirt, and blood. "I'm as big as you now, an'
I'm goin' to git bigger. Then I'll lick you—see if I don't."

"You ought to be to work, seein' how big you are," Johnny
snarled. "That's what's the matter with you. You ought
to be to work. An' it's up to your ma to put you to work."

"But he's too young," she protested. "He's only a little
boy."

"I was younger'n him when I started to work."

Johnny's mouth was open, further to express the sense of
unfairness that he felt, but the mouth closed with a snap.
He turned gloomily on his heel and stalked into the house
and to bed. The door of his room was open to let in warmth

from the kitchen. As he undressed in the semi-darkness he could hear his mother talking with a neighbor woman who had dropped in. His mother was crying, and her speech was punctuated with spiritless sniffles.

"I can't make out what's gittin' into Johnny," he could hear her say. "He didn't used to be this way. He was a patient little angel."

"An' he is a good boy," she hastened to defend. "He's worked faithful, an' he did go to work too young. But it wasn't my fault. I do the best I can, I'm sure."

Prolonged sniffling from the kitchen, and Johnny murmured to himself as his eyelids closed down, "You betcher life I've worked faithful."

The next morning he was torn bodily by his mother from the grip of sleep. Then came the meagre breakfast, the tramp through the dark, and the pale glimpse of day across the housetops as he turned his back on it and went in through the factory gate. It was another day, of all the days, and all the days were alike.

And yet there had been variety in his life—at the times he changed from one job to another, or was taken sick. When he was six, he was little mother and father to Will and the other children still younger. At seven he went into the mills—winding bobbins. When he was eight, he got work in another mill. His new job was marvellously easy. All he had to do was to sit down with a little stick in his hand and guide a stream of cloth that flowed past him. This stream of cloth came out of the maw of a machine, passed over a hot roller, and went on its way elsewhere. But he sat always in the one place, beyond the reach of daylight, a gas-jet flaring over him, himself part of the mechanism.

He was very happy at that job, in spite of the moist heat, for he was still young and in possession of dreams and illusions. And wonderful dreams he dreamed as he watched the steaming cloth streaming endlessly by. But there was no exercise about the work, no call upon his mind, and he dreamed less and less, while his mind grew torpid and drowsy.

Nevertheless, he earned two dollars a week, and two dollars represented the difference between acute starvation and chronic underfeeding.

But when he was nine, he lost his job. Measles was the cause of it. After he recovered, he got work in a glass factory. The pay was better, and the work demanded skill. It was piece-work, and the more skillful he was, the bigger wages he earned. Here was incentive. And under this incentive he developed into a remarkable worker.

It was simple work, the tying of glass stoppers into small bottles. At his waist he carried a bundle of twine. He held the bottles between his knees so that he might work with both hands. Thus, in a sitting position and bending over his own knees, his narrow shoulders grew humped and his chest was contracted for ten hours each day. This was not good for the lungs, but he tied three hundred dozen bottles a day.

The superintendent was very proud of him, and brought visitors to look at him. In ten hours three hundred dozen bottles passed through his hands. This meant that he had attained machine-like perfection. All waste movements were eliminated. Every motion of his thin arms, every movement of a muscle in the thin fingers, was swift and accurate. He worked at high tension, and the result was that he grew nervous. At night his muscles twitched in his sleep, and in the daytime he could not relax and rest. He remained keyed up and his muscles continued to twitch. Also he grew sallow and his lint-cough grew worse. Then pneumonia laid hold of the feeble lungs within the contracted chest, and he lost his job in the glassworks.

Now he had returned to the jute mills where he had first begun with winding bobbins. But promotion was waiting for him. He was a good worker. He would next go on the starcher, and later he would go into the loom room. There was nothing after that except increased efficiency.

The machinery ran faster than when he had first gone to

work, and his mind ran slower. He no longer dreamed at all, though his earlier years had been full of dreaming. Once he had been in love. It was when he first began guiding the cloth over the hot roller, and it was with the daughter of the superintendent. She was much older than he, a young woman, and he had seen her at a distance only a paltry half-dozen times. But that made no difference. On the surface of the cloth stream that poured past him, he pictured radiant futures wherein he performed prodigies of toil, invented miraculous machines, won to the mastership of the mills, and in the end took her in his arms and kissed her soberly on the brow.

But that was all in the long ago, before he had grown too old and tired to love. Also, she had married and gone away, and his mind had gone to sleep. Yet it had been a wonderful experience, and he used often to look back upon it as other men and women look back upon the time they believed in fairies. He had never believed in fairies nor Santa Claus; but he had believed implicitly in the smiling future his imagination had wrought into the steaming cloth stream.

He had become a man very early in life. At seven, when he drew his first wages, began his adolescence. A certain feeling of independence. A certain feeling of independence crept up in him, and the relationship between him and his mother changed. Somehow, as an earner and breadwinner, doing his own work in the world, he was more like an equal with her. Manhood, full-blown manhood, had come when he was eleven, at which time he had gone to work on the night shift for six months. No child works on the night shift and remains a child.

There had been several great events in his life. One of these had been when his mother bought some California prunes. Two others had been the two times when she cooked custard. Those had been events. He remembered them kindly. And at that time his mother had told him of a blissful dish she would sometime make—"floating island," she had called it, "better than custard." For years he had looked forward to the day when he would sit down to the table with floating island before him, until at last he had relegated the idea of it to the limbo of unattainable ideals.

Once he found a silver quarter lying on the sidewalk. That, also, was a great event in his life, withal a tragic one. He knew his duty on the instant the silver flashed on his eyes, before even he had picked it up. At home, as usual, there was not enough to eat, and home he should have taken it as he did his wages every Saturday night. Right conduct in this case was obvious; but he never had any spending of his money, and he was suffering from candy hunger. He was ravenous for the sweets that only on red-letter days he had ever tasted in his life.

He did not attempt to deceive himself. He knew it was sin, and deliberately he sinned when he went on a fifteen-cent candy debauch. Ten cents he saved for a future orgy; but not being accustomed to the carrying of money, he lost the ten cents. This occurred at the time when he was suffering all the torments of conscience, and it was to him an act of divine retribution. He had a frightened sense of the closeness of an awful and wrathful God. God had seen, and God had been swift to punish, denying him even the full wages of sin.

In memory he always looked back upon that event as the one great criminal deed of his life, and at the recollection his conscience always awoke and gave him another twinge. It was the one skeleton in his closet. Also, being so made and circumstanced, he looked back upon the deed with regret. He was dissatisfied with the manner in which he had spent the quarter. He could have invested it better, and, out of his later knowledge of the quickness of God, he would have beaten God out by spending the whole quarter at one fell swoop. In restrospect he spent the quarter a thousand times, and each time to better advantage.

There was one other memory of the past, dim and faded, but stamped into his soul everlastingly by the savage feet of his father. It was more like a nightmare than a remembered

vision of a concrete thing—more like the race-memory of
man that makes him fall in his sleep and that goes back to
his arboreal ancestry.

This particular memory never came to Johnny in broad
daylight when he was wide awake. It came at night, in bed,
at the moment that his consciousness was sinking down and
losing itself in sleep. It always aroused him to frightened
wakefulness, and for the moment, in the first sickening start,
it seemed to him that he lay crosswise on the foot of the
bed. In the bed were the vague forms of his father and
mother. He never saw what his father looked like. He had
but one impression of his father, and that was that he had
savage and pitiless feet.

His earlier memories lingered with him, but he had no late
memories. All days were alike. Yesterday or last year were
the same as a thousand years—or a minute. Nothing ever
happened. There were no events to mark the march of time.
Time did not march. It stood always still. It was only the
whirling machines that moved, and they moved nowhere—
in spite of the fact that they moved faster.

When he was fourteen, he went to work on the starcher.
It was a colossal event. Something had at last happened that
could be remembered beyond a night's sleep or a week's pay-
day. It marked an era. It was a machine Olympiad, a thing
to date from. "When I went to work on the starcher," or,
"after," or "before I went to work on the starcher," were
sentences often on his lips.

He celebrated his sixteenth birthday by going into the loom
room and taking a loom. Here was an incentive again, for
it was piece-work. And he excelled, because the clay of him
had been moulded by the mills into the perfect machine. At
the end of three months he was running two looms, and, later,
three and four.

At the end of his second year at the looms he was turning
out more yards than any other weaver, and more than twice
as much as some of the less skillful ones. And at home things
began to prosper as he approached the full stature of his earn-

ing power. Not, however, that his increased earnings were in excess of need. The children were growing up. They ate more. And they were going to school, and schoolbooks cost money. And somehow, the faster he worked, the faster climbed the prices of things. Even the rent went up, though the house had fallen from bad to worse disrepair.

He had grown taller; but with his increased height he seemed leaner than ever. Also, he was more nervous. With the nervousness increased peevishness and irritability. The children had learned by many bitter lessons to fight shy of him. His mother respected him for his earning power, but somehow her respect was tinctured with fear.

There was no joyousness in life for him. The procession of the days he never saw. The nights he slept away in twitching unconsciousness. The rest of the time he worked, and his consciousness was machine consciousness. Outside this his mind was a blank. He had no ideals, and but one illusion; namely, that he drank excellent coffee. He was a workbeast. He had no mental life whatever; yet deep down in the crypts of his mind, unknown to him, were being weighed and sifted every hour in his toil, every movement of his hands, every twitch of his muscles, and preparations were making for a future course of action that would amaze him and all his little world.

It was in the late spring that he came home from work one night aware of unusual tiredness. There was a keen expectancy in the air as he sat down to the table, but he did not notice. He went through the meal in moody silence, mechanically eating what was before him. The children um'd and ah'd and made smacking noises with their mouths. But he was deaf to them.

"D'ye know what you're eatin'?" his mother demanded at last, desperately.

He looked vacantly at the dish before him, and vacantly at her.

"Floatin' island," she announced triumphantly.

"Oh," he said.

"Floating island!" the children chorused loudly.

"Oh," he said. And after two or three mouthfuls, he added, "I guess I ain't hungry to-night."

He dropped the spoon, shoved back his chair, and arose wearily from the table.

"An' I guess I'll go to bed."

His feet dragged more heavily than usual as he crossed the kitchen floor. Undressing was a Titan's task, a monstrous futility, and he wept weakly as he crawled into bed, one shoe still on. He was aware of a rising, swelling something inside his head that made his brain thick and fuzzy. His lean fingers felt as big as his wrist, while in the ends of them was a remoteness of sensation vague and fuzzy like his brain. The small of his back ached intolerably. All his bones ached. He ached everywhere. And in his head began the shrieking, pounding, crashing, roaring of a million looms. All space was filled with flying shuttles. They darted in and out, intricately, amongst the stars. He worked a thousand looms himself, and ever they speeded up, faster and faster, and his brain unwound, faster and faster, and became the thread that fed the thousand flying shuttles.

He did not go to work next morning. He was too busy weaving colossally on the thousand looms that ran inside his head. His mother went to work, but first she sent for the doctor. It was a severe attack of la grippe, he said. Jennie served as nurse and carried out his instructions.

It was a very severe attack, and it was a week before Johnny dressed and tottered feebly across the floor. Another week, the doctor said, and he would be fit to return to work. The foreman of the loom room visited him on Sunday afternoon, the first day of his convalescence. The best weaver in the room, the foreman told his mother. His job would be held for him. He could come back to work a week from Monday.

"Why don't you thank 'im, Johnny?" his mother asked anxiously.

"He's ben that sick he ain't himself yet," she explained apologetically to the visitor.

Johnny sat hunched up and gazing steadfastly at the floor. He sat in the same position long after the foreman had gone. It was warm outdoors, and he sat on the stoop in the afternoon. Sometimes his lips moved. He seemed lost in endless calculations.

Next morning, after the day grew warm, he took his seat on the stoop. He had pencil and paper this time with which to continue his calculations, and he calculated painfully and amazingly.

"What comes after millions?" he asked at noon, when Will came home from school. "An' how d'ye work 'em?"

That afternoon finished his task. Each day, but without paper and pencil, he returned to the stoop. He was greatly absorbed in the one tree that grew across the street. He studied it for hours at a time, and was unusually interested when the wind swayed its branches and fluttered its leaves. Throughout the week he seemed lost in a great communion with himself. On Sunday, sitting on the stoop, he laughed aloud, several times, to the perturbation of his mother, who had not heard him laugh in years.

Next morning, in the early darkness, she came to his bed to rouse him. He had had his fill of sleep all week, and awoke easily. He made no struggle, nor did he attempt to hold on to the bedding when she stripped it from him. He lay quietly, and spoke quietly.

"It ain't no use, ma."

"You'll be late," she said, under the impression that he was still stupid with sleep.

"I'm awake, ma, an' I tell you it ain't no use. You might as well lemme alone. I ain't goin' to git up."

"But you'll lose your job!" she cried.

"I ain't goin' to git up," he repeated in a strange, passionless voice.

She did not go to work herself that morning. This was sickness beyond any sickness she had ever known. Fever and delirium she could understand; but this was insanity. She pulled the bedding up over him and sent Jennie for the doctor.

When that person arrived Johnny was sleeping gently, and gently he awoke and allowed his pulse to be taken.

"Nothing the matter with him," the doctor reported. "Badly debilitated, that's all. Not much meat on his bones."

"He's always been that way," his mother volunteered.

"Now go 'way, ma, an' let me finish my snooze."

Johnny spoke sweetly and placidly, and sweetly and placidly he rolled over on his side and went to sleep.

At ten o'clock he awoke and dressed himself. He walked out into the kitchen, where he found his mother with a frightened expression on her face.

"I'm goin' away, ma," he announced, "an' I jes' want to say good-by."

She threw her apron over her head and sat down suddenly and wept. He waited patiently.

"I might a-known it," she was sobbing.

"Where?" she finally asked, removing the apron from her head and gazing up at him with a stricken face in which there was little curiosity.

"I don't know—anywhere."

As he spoke, the tree across the street appeared with dazzling brightness on his inner vision. It seemed to lurk just under his eyelids, and he could see it whenever he wished.

"An' your job?" she quavered.

"I ain't never goin' to work again."

"My God, Johnny!" she wailed, "don't say that!"

What he had said was blasphemy to her. As a mother who hears her child deny God, was Johnny's mother shocked by his words.

"What's got into you, anyway?" she demanded, with a lame attempt at imperativeness.

"Figures," he answered. "Jes' figures. I've ben doin' a lot of figurin' this week, an' it's most surprisin'."

"I don't see what that's got to do with it," she sniffled.

Johnny smiled patiently, and his mother was aware of a distinct shock at the persistent absence of his peevishness and irritability.

"I'll show you," he said. "I'm plum' tired out. What makes me tired? Moves. I've ben moving' ever since I was born. I'm tired of movin', an' I ain't goin' to move any more. Remember when I worked in the glass-house? I used to do three hundred dozen a day. Now I reckon I made about ten different moves to each bottle. That's thirty-six thousan' moves a day. Ten days, three hundred an' sixty thousan' moves a day. One month, one million an' eighty thousan' moves. Chuck out the eighty thousan'—" he spoke with the complacent beneficence of a philanthropist—"chuck out the eighty thousan', that leaves a million moves a month —twelve million moves a year.

"At the looms I'm movin' twic'st as much. That makes twenty-five million moves a year, an' it seems to me I've ben a-movin' that way 'most a million years.

"Now this week I ain't moved at all. I ain't made one move in hours an' hours. I tell you it was swell, jes' settin' there, hours an' hours, an' doin' nothin'. I ain't never ben happy before. I never had any time. I've ben movin' all the time. That ain't no way to be happy. An' I ain't goin' to do it any more. I'm jes' goin' to set, an' set, an' rest, an' rest, and then rest some more."

"But what's goin' to come of Will an' the children?" she asked despairingly.

"That's it, 'Will an' the children,' " he repeated.

But there was no bitterness in his voice. He had long known his mother's ambition for the younger boy, but the thought of it no longer rankled. Nothing mattered any more. Not even that.

"I know, ma, what you've ben plannin' for Will—keepin' him in school to make a bookkeeper out of him. But it ain't no use, I've quit. He's got to go to work."

"An' after I have brung you up the way I have," she

wept, starting to cover her head with the apron and changing her mind.

"You never brung me up," he answered with sad kindli-
ness. "I brung myself up, ma, an' I brung up Will. He's
bigger'n me, an' heavier an' taller. When I was a kid, I
reckon I didn't git enough to eat. When he come along an'
was a kid, I was workin' an' earnin' grub for him too. But
that's done with. Will can go to work, same as me, or he
can go to hell, I don't care which. I'm tired. I'm goin'
now. Ain't you goin' to say good-by?"

She made no reply. The apron had gone over her head
again, and she was crying. He paused a moment in the door-
way.

"I'm sure I done the best I knew how," she was sobbing.

He passed out of the house and down the street. A wan
delight came into his face at the sight of the lone tree. "Jes'
ain't goin' to do nothin'," he said to himself, half aloud, in
a crooning tone. He glanced wistfully up at the sky, but
the bright sun dazzled and blinded him.

It was a long walk he took, and he did not walk fast. It
took him past the jute-mill. The muffled roar of the looms
came to his ears, and he smiled. It was a gentle, placid
smile. He hated no one, not even the pounding, shrieking
machines. There was no bitterness in him, nothing but an
inordinate hunger for rest.

The houses and factories thinned out and the open spaces
increased as he approached the country. At last the city
was behind him, and he was walking down a leafy lane beside the railroad track. He did not walk like a man. He
did not look like a man. He was a travesty of the human.
It was a twisted and stunted and nameless piece of life that
shambled like a sickly ape, arms loose-hanging, stoop-shoul-
dered, narrow-chested, grotesque and terrible.

He passed by a small railroad station and lay down in the
grass under a tree. All afternoon he lay there. Sometimes
he dozed, with muscles that twitched in his sleep. When

awake, he lay without movement, watching the birds or looking up at the sky through the branches of the tree above him. Once or twice he laughed aloud, but without relevance to anything he had seen or felt.

After twilight had gone, in the first darkness of the night, a freight train rumbled into the station. When the engine was switching cars on to the sidetrack, Johnny crept along the side of the train. He pulled open the side-door of an empty box-car and awkwardly and laboriously climbed in. He closed the door. The engine whistled. Johnny was lying down, and in the darkness he smiled.

THE DREAM OF DEBS

THE DREAM OF DEBS

I AWOKE fully an hour before my customary time. This in itself was remarkable, and I lay very wide awake, pondering over it. Something was the matter, something was wrong—I knew not what. I was oppressed by a premonition of something terrible that had happened or was about to happen. But what was it? I strove to orientate myself. I remembered that at the time of the Great Earthquake of 1906 many claimed they awakened some moments before the first shock and that during those moments they experienced strange feelings of dread. Was San Francisco again to be visited by earthquake?

I lay for a full minute, numbly expectant, but there occurred no reeling of walls nor shock and grind of falling masonry. All was quiet. That was it! The silence! No wonder I had been perturbed. The hum of the great live city was strangely silent. The surface cars passed along my street at that time of day, on an average of one every three minutes; but in the ten succeeding minutes not a car passed. Perhaps it was a street railway strike, was my thought; or perhaps there had been an accident and the power was shut off. But no, the silence was too profound. I heard no jar and rattle of wagon-wheels, nor stamp of iron-shod hoofs straining up the steep cobblestones.

Pressing the push-button beside my bed, I strove to hear the sound of the bell, though I knew it was impossible for the sound to rise three stories to me even if the bell did ring. It rang all right, for a few minutes later Brown entered with the tray and morning paper. Though his features were impassive as ever, I noted a startled, apprehensive light in his eyes. I noted, also, that there was no cream on the tray.

"The creamery did not deliver this morning," he explained; "nor did the bakery."

I glanced again at the tray. There were no fresh French rolls—only slices of stale graham bread from yesterday, the most detestable of bread so far as I was concerned.

"Nothing was delivered this morning, sir." Brown started to explain apologetically; but I interrupted him.

"The paper?"

"Yes, sir, it was delivered, but it was the only thing, and it is the last time, too. There won't be any paper tomorrow. The paper says so. Can I send out and get you some condensed milk?"

I shook my head, accepted the coffee black, and spread open the paper. The headlines explained everything—explained too much, in fact, for the lengths of pessimism to which the journal went, were ridiculous. A general strike, it said, had been called all over the United States; and most foreboding anxieties were expressed concerning the provisioning of the great cities.

I read on hastily, skimming much and remembering much of the labor troubles in the past. For a generation the general strike had been the dream of organized labor, which dream had arisen originally in the mind of Debs, one of the great leaders of thirty years before. I recollected that in my young college-settlement days I had even written an article on the subject for one of the magazines and that I had entitled it, "The Dream of Debs." And I must confess that I had treated the idea very carefully and academically as a dream and nothing more. Time and the world had rolled on, Gompers was gone, the American Federation of Labor was gone, and gone was Debs with all his wild revolutionary ideas; but the dream had persisted, and here it was at last realized in fact. But I laughed, as I read, at the journal's gloomy outlook. I knew better. I had seen organized labor worsted in too many conflicts. It would be a matter only of days when the thing would be settled. This was a national strike, and it wouldn't take the government long to break it.

I threw the paper down and proceeded to dress. It would certainly be interesting to be out in the streets of San Francisco when not a wheel was turning and the whole city was taking an enforced vacation.

"I beg your pardon, sir," Brown said, as he handed me my cigar case, "but Mr. Harmmed has asked to see you before you go out."

"Send him in right away," I answered.

Harmmed was the butler. When he entered I could see he was laboring under controlled excitement. He came at once to the point.

"What shall I do, sir? There will be needed provisions, and the delivery drivers are on strike. And the electricity is shut off—I guess they're on strike, too."

"Are the shops open?" I asked.

"Only the small ones, sir. The retail clerks are out and the big ones can't open; but the owners and their families are running the little ones themselves."

"Then take the machine," I said, "and go the rounds and make your purchases. Buy plenty of everything you need or may need. Get a box of candles—no, get half a dozen boxes. And when you're done, tell Harrison to bring the machine around to the club for me—not later than eleven."

Harmmed shook his head gravely. "Mr. Harrison has struck along with the Chauffeurs' Union, and I don't know how to run the machine myself."

"Oh, ho, he has, has he?" I said. "Well, when next Mister Harrison happens around you tell him that he can look elsewhere for a position."

"Yes, sir."

"You don't happen to belong to a Butler's Union, do you Harmmed?

"No, sir," was the answer. "And even if I did I'd not desert my employer in a crisis like this. No, sir, I would—"

"All right, thank you," I said. "Now you get ready to accompany me. I'll run the machine myself, and we'll lay in a stock of provisions to stand a siege."

It was a beautiful first of May, even as May days go. The sky was cloudless, there was no wind, and the air was warm —almost balmy. Many autos were out, but the owners were driving them themselves. The streets were crowded but quiet. The working class, dressed in its Sunday best, was out taking the air and observing the effects of the strike. It was all so unusual, and withal so peaceful, that I found myself enjoying it. My nerves were tinkling with mild excitement. It was a sort of placid adventure. I passed Miss Chickering. She was at the helm of her little runabout. She swung around and came after me, catching me at the corner.

"Oh, Mr. Cerf!" she hailed. "Do you know where I can buy candles? I've been to a dozen shops, and they're all sold out. It's dreadfully awful, isn't it?"

But her sparkling eyes gave the lie to her words. Like the rest of us, she was enjoying it hugely. Quite an adventure it was, getting those candles. It was not until we went across the city and down into the working class quarter south of Market street that we found small corner groceries that had not yet sold out. Miss Chickering thought one box was sufficient, but I persuaded her into taking four. My car was large, and I laid in a dozen boxes. There was no telling what delays might arise in the settlement of the strike. Also I filled the car with sacks of flour, baking powder, tinned goods, and all the ordinary necessaries of life suggested by Harmmed, who fussed around and clucked over the purchases like an anxious old hen.

The remarkable thing, that first day of the strike, was that no one really apprehended anything serious. The announcement of organized labor in the morning papers that it was prepared to stay out a month or three months was laughed at. And yet that very first day we might have guessed as much from the fact that the working class took practically no part in the great rush to buy provisions. Of course not. For weeks and months, craftily and secretly, the whole working class had been laying in private stocks of provisions. That was why we were permitted to go down and buy out the little groceries in the working class neighborhood.

It was not until I arrived at the Club that afternoon that I began to feel the first alarm. Everything was in confusion. There were no olives for the cocktails, and the service was by hitches and jerks. Most of the men were angry, and all were worried. A babel of voices greeted me as I entered. General Folsom, nursing his capacious paunch in a window-seat in the smoking-room, was defending himself against half a dozen excited gentlemen who were demanding that he do something.

"What can I do more than I have done?" he was saying. "There are no orders from Washington. If you gentlemen will get a wire through I'll do anything I am commanded to do. But I don't see what can be done. The first thing I did this morning, as soon as I learned of the strike, was to order in the troops from the Presidio—three thousand of them. They're guarding the banks, the mint, the post office, and all the public buildings. There is no disorder whatever. The strikers are keeping the peace perfectly. You can't expect me to shoot them down as they walk along the streets with wives and children all in their best bib and tucker."

"I'd like to know what's happening on Wall street," I heard Jimmy Wombold say as I passed along. I could imagine his anxiety, for I knew that he was deep in the big Consolidated-Western deal.

"Say, Cerf," Atkinson bustled up to me, "Is your machine running?"

"Yes," I answered, "but what's the matter with your own?"

"Broken down, and the garages are all closed. And my wife's somewhere around Truckee, I think, stalled on the Overland. Can't get a wire to her for love or money. She should have arrived this evening. She may be starving. Lend me your machine."

"Can't get it across the bay," Halsted spoke up. "The ferries aren't running. But I tell you what you can do.

There's Rollinson—oh, Rollinson, come here a moment. Atkinson wants to get a machine across the bay. His wife is stuck on the Overland at Truckee. Can't you bring the 'Lurlette' across from Tiburon and carry the machine over for him?"

The "Lurlette" was a two-hundred-ton ocean-going schooner-yacht.

Rollinson shook his head. "You couldn't get a longshoreman to load the machine on board, even if I could get the 'Lurlette' over, which I can't for the crew are members of the Coast Seamen's Union, and they're on strike along with the rest."

"But my wife may be starving." I could hear Atkinson wailing as I moved on.

At the other end of the smoking room I ran into a group of men bunched excitedly and angrily around Bertie Messener. And Bertie was stirring them up and prodding them in his cool, cynical way. Bertie didn't care about the strike. He didn't care much about anything. He was blasé—at least in all the clean things of life; the nasty things had no attraction for him. He was worth twenty millions, all of it in safe investments, and he had never done a tap of productive work in his life—inherited it all from his father and two uncles. He had been everywhere, seen everything, and done everything but get married, and this last in the face of the grim and determined attack of a few hundred ambitious mammas. For years he had been the greatest catch, and as yet he had avoided being caught. He was disgracefully eligible. On top of his wealth, he was young and handsome, and, as I said before, clean. He was a great athlete, a young blond god that did everything perfectly and admirably with the solitary exception of matrimony. And he didn't care about anything, had no ambitions, no passions, no desire to do the very things he did so much better than other men.

"This is sedition!" one man in the group was crying. Another called it revolt and revolution, and another called it anarchy.

"I can't see it," Bertie said. "I have been out in the streets all morning. Perfect order reigns. I never saw a more law-abiding populace. There's no use calling it names. It's not any of these things. It's just what it claims to be, a general strike, and it's your turn to play, gentlemen."

"And we'll play alright!" cried Garfield, one of the traction millionaires. "We'll show this dirt where its place is—the beasts! Wait till the government takes a hand."

"But where is the government?" Bertie interposed. "It might as well be at the bottom of the sea so far as you're concerned. You don't know what's happening at Washington. You don't know whether you've got a government or not."

"Don't you worry about that!" Garfield blurted out.

"I assure you I'm not worrying," Bertie smiled languidly. "But it seems to me it's what you fellows are doing. Look in the glass, Garfield."

Garfield did not look, for had he looked, he would have seen a very excited gentleman with rumpled, iron-gray hair, a flushed face, mouth sullen and vindictive, and eyes wildly gleaming.

"It's not right, I tell you," little Hanover said; and from his tone I was sure that he had already said it a number of times.

"Now, that's going too far, Hanover," Bertie replied. "You fellows make me tired. You're all open-shop men. You've eroded my eardrums with your endless gabble for the open-shop and the right of a man to work. You've har-angued along those lines for years. Labor is doing nothing wrong in going out on this general strike. It is violating no law of God nor man. Don't you talk, Hanover. You've been ringing the changes too long on the God-given right to work . . . . or not to work; you can't escape the corollary. It's a dirty little sordid scrap, that's all the whole thing is. You've got labor down and gouged it, and now labor's got you down and is gouging you, that's all, and you're squealing."

Every man in the group broke out in indignant denials that labor had ever been gouged.

"No, sir!" Garfield was shouting, "we've done the best for labor. Instead of gouging it, we've given it a chance to live. We've made work for it. Where would labor be if it hadn't been for us?"

"A whole lot better off," Bertie sneered. "You've got labor down and gouged it every time you got a chance, and you went out of your way to make chances."

"No! No!" were the cries.

"There was the teamster's strike right here in San Francisco," Bertie went on imperturbably. "The Employers' Association precipitated that strike. You know that. And you know I know it, too, for I've sat in these very rooms and heard the inside talk and news of the fight. First you precipitated the strike, then you bought the Mayor and the Chief of Police and broke the strike. A pretty spectacle, you philanthropists getting the teamsters down and gouging them.

"Hold on, I'm not through with you. It's only last year that the labor ticket of Colorado elected a Governor. He was never seated. You know why. You know how your brother philanthropists and capitalists of Colorado worked it. It was a case of getting labor down and gouging it. You kept the President of the Southwestern Amalgamated Association of Miners in jail for three years on trumped up murder charges, and with him out of the way you broke up the Association. That was gouging labor; you'll admit. The third time the graduated income tax was declared unconstitutional was a gouge. So was the Eight-hour Bill you killed in the last Congress.

"And of all the unmitigated immoral gouges, your destruction of the closed-shop principle was the limit. You know how it was done. You bought out Farburg, the last president of the old American Federation of Labor. He was your creature—or the creature of all the trusts and employers' associations, which is the same thing. You precipitated the big

Closed Shop Strike. Farburg betrayed that strike. You won, and the old American Federation of Labor crumbled to pieces. You fellows destroyed it, and by so doing undid yourselves; for right on top of it began the organization of the I. L. W. —the biggest and solidest organization of labor the United States has ever seen, and you are responsible for its existence and for the present general strike. You smashed all the old federations and drove labor into the I. L. W., and the I. L. W., called the general strike — still fighting for the closed shop. And then you have the effrontery to stand here face to face and tell me that you never got labor down and gouged it. Bah!!"

This time there was no denials. Garfield broke out in self-defense:

"We've done nothing we were not compelled to do, if we were to win."

"I'm not saying anything about that," Bertie answered. "What I am complaining about is your squealing now that you're getting a taste of your own medicine. How many strikes have you won by starving labor into submission? Well, labor's worked out a scheme whereby to starve you into submission. It wants the closed shop, and if it can get it by starving you, starve you shall."

"I notice that you have profited in the past by those very labor-gouges you mentioned," insinuated Brentwood, one of the wiliest and most astute of our corporation lawyers. "The receiver is as bad as the thief," he sneered. "You had no hand in the gouging, but you took your whack out of the gouge."

"That is quite beside the question, Brentwood," Bertie drawled. "You're as bad as Hanover, intruding the moral element. I haven't said that anything is right or wrong. It's all a rotten game, I know; and my sole kick is that you fellows are squealing now that you're down and labor's taking a gouge out of you. Of course I've taken the profits from the gouging, and, thanks to you, gentlemen, without having personally to do the dirty work. You did that for me—oh, believe me, not because I am more virtuous than you, but because my good father and his various brothers left me a lot of money with which to pay for the dirty work."

"If you mean to insinuate—" Brentwood began hotly.

"Hold on, don't get all ruffled up," Bertie interposed insolently. "There's no use in playing hypocrites in this thieves' den. The high and lofty is all right for the newspapers, boys' clubs and Sunday schools—that's part of the game; but for heaven's sake, don't let's play it on one another. You know, and you know I know, just what jobbery was done in the building trades' strike last fall, who put up the money, who did the work, and who profited by it." (Brentwood flushed darkly.) "But we are all tarred with the same brush, and the best thing for us to do is to leave the morality out of it. Again I repeat, play the game, play it to the last finish, but for goodness sake, don't squeal when you get hurt."

When I left the group Bertie was off on a new tack, tormenting them with the more serious aspects of the situation, pointing out the shortage of supplies that was already making itself felt, and asking them what they were going to do about it. A little later I met him in the cloak room, leaving, and gave him a lift home in my machine.

"It's a great stroke, this general strike," he said, as we bowled along through the crowded but orderly streets. "It's a smashing body-blow. Labor caught us napping and struck at our weakest place, the stomach. I'm going to get out of San Francisco, Cerf. Take my advice and get out, too. Head for the country, anywhere. You'll have more chance. Buy up a stock of supplies and get into a tent or cabin somewhere. Soon there'll be nothing but starvation in this city for such as we."

How correct Bertie Messener was, I never dreamed. I decided mentally that he was an alarmist. As for myself I was content to remain and watch the fun. After I dropped him, instead of going directly home, I went on in a hunt for more food. To my surprise, I learned that the small groceries where I had bought in the morning were sold out. I extended my search to the Potrero, and by good luck managed to pick up another box of candles, two sacks of wheat flour, ten pounds of graham flour (which would do for the servants), a case of tinned corn, and two cases of tinned tomatoes. It did look as though there was going to be at least a temporary food shortage, and I hugged myself over the goodly stock of provisions I had laid in.

The next morning I had my coffee in bed as usual, and, more than the cream, I missed the daily paper. It was this absence of knowledge of what was going on in the world that I found the chiefest hardship. Down at the club there was little news. Rider had crossed from Oakland in his launch, and Halsted had been down to San José and back in his machine. They reported the same condition in those places as in San Francisco. Everything was tied up by the strike. All grocery stocks had been bought out by the upper classes. And perfect order reigned. But what was happening over the rest of the country—in Chicago? New York? Washington? Most probably the same things that were happening with us, we concluded; but the fact that we did not know with absolute surety was irritating.

General Folsom had a bit of news. An attempt had been made to place army telegraphers in the telegraph offices, but the wires had been cut in every direction. This was, so far, the one unlawful act committed by labor, and that it was a concerted act he was fully convinced. He had communicated by wireless with the army post at Benicia, the telegraph lines were even then being patrolled by soldiers all the way to Sacramento. Once, for one short instant, they had got the Sacramento call, then the wires, somewhere, were cut again. General Folsom reasoned that similar attempts to open communication were being made by the authorities all the way across the continent, but he was non-committal as to whether or not he thought the attempt would succeed. What worried him was the wire-cutting, he could not but believe that it was an important part of the deep-laid labor conspiracy. Also, he regretted that the government had not long since established its projected chain of wireless stations.

The days came and went, and for a time it was a humdrum time. Nothing happened. The edge of excitement had become blunted. The streets were not so crowded. The working class did not come up town any more to see how we were taking the strike. And there were not so many automobiles running around. The repair shops and garages were closed, and whenever a machine broke down it went out of commission. The clutch on mine broke and love nor money could not get it repaired. Like the rest, I now was walking. San Francisco lay dead, and we did not know what was happening over the rest of the country. But from the very fact that we did not know we could conclude only that the rest of the country lay as dead as San Francisco. From time to time the city was placarded with the proclamations of organized labor—these had been printed months before and evidenced how thoroughly the I. L. W. had prepared for the strike. Every detail had been worked out long in advance. No violence had occurred as yet, with the exception of the shooting of a few wire-cutters by the soldiers, but the people of the slums were starving and growing ominously restless.

The business men, the millionaires, and the professional class held meetings and passed proclamations, but there was no way of making the proclamations public. They could not even get them printed. One result of these meetings, however, was that General Folsom was persuaded into taking military possession of the wholesale houses and of all the flour, grain and food warehouses. It was high time, for suffering was becoming acute in the homes of the rich, and breadlines were necessary. I know that my servants were beginning to draw long faces, and it was amazing—the hole they made in my stock of provisions. In fact, as I afterward surmised, each servant was stealing from me and secreting a private stock of provisions for himself.

But with the formation of the bread lines came new troubles. There was only so much of a food reserve in San Francisco, and at the best it could not last long. Organized labor, we knew, had its private supplies; nevertheless, the whole working class joined the bread lines. As a result, the provisions General Folsom had taken possession of diminished with perilous rapidity. How were the soldiers going to distinguish between a shabby middle-class man, a member of the I. L. W., or a slum-dweller? The first and the last had to be fed, but the soldiers did not know all the I. L. W. men in the city, much less the wives and sons and daughters of the I. L. W. men. The employers helping, a few of the known union men were flung out of the bread lines; but that amounted to nothing. To make matters worse, the government tugs that had been hauling food from the army depots on Mare Island to Angel Island found no more food to haul. The soldiers now received their rations from the confiscated provisions, and they received them first.

The beginning of the end was in sight. Violence was beginning to show its awful face. Law and order were passing away, and passing away, I must confess, among the slum people and the upper classes. Organized labor still maintained perfect order. It could well afford to—it had plenty to eat. I remember the afternoon at the Club when I caught Halsted and Brentwood whispering in a corner. They took me in on the venture. Brentwood's machine was still in running order, and they were going out cow-stealing. Halsted had a long butcher-knife and a cleaver. We went out to the outskirts of the city. Here and there were cows grazing, but always guarded by their owners. We pursued our quest, following along the fringe of the city to the east, and on the hills near Hunter's Point we came upon a cow guarded by a little girl. There was also a young calf with the cow. We wasted no time on preliminaries. The little girl ran away screaming, while we slaughtered the cow. I omit the details, for they are not nice—we were unaccustomed to such work, and we bungled it.

But in the midst of it, working with the haste of fear, we heard cries, and we saw a number of men running toward us. We abandoned the spoils and took to our heels. To our surprise we were not pursued. Looking back, we saw the men hurriedly cutting up the cow. They had been on the same lay as ourselves. We argued that there was plenty for all, and ran back. The scene that followed beggars description. We fought and squabbled over the division like savages. Brentwood, I remember, was a perfect brute, snarling and snapping and threatening that murder would be done if we did not get our proper share.

And we were getting our share when there occurred a new irruption on the scene. This time it was the dreaded peace officers of the I. L. W. The little girl had brought them. They were armed with whips and clubs, and there were a score of them. The little girl danced up and down in anger, the tears streaming down her cheeks, crying, "Give it to 'em! Give it to 'em! That guy with the specs—he did it! Mash his face for him! Mash his face!" That guy with the specs was I and I got my face mashed, too, though I had the presence of mind to take off my glasses at the first. My! but we did receive a trouncing as we scattered in all directions. Brentwood, Halstead and I flew away for the machine. Brentwood's nose was bleeding, while Halstead's cheek was cut across with the scarlet slash of a blacksnake whip.

And lo, when the pursuit ceased and we had gained the machine, there, hiding behind it, was the frightened calf. Brentwood warned us to be cautious and crept upon it like a wolf or tiger. Knife and cleaver had been left behind, but Brentwood still had his hands, and over and over on the ground he rolled with the poor little calf as he throttled it. We threw the carcass into the machine, covered it over with a robe, and started home. But our misfortunes had only begun. We blew out a tire. There was no way of fixing it, and twilight was coming on. We abandoned the machine, Brentwood puffing and staggering along in advance, the calf, covered by the robe, slung across his shoulders. We took turn about carrying that calf, and it nearly killed us. Also we lost our way. And then, after hours of wandering and toil, we encountered a gang of hoodlums. They were not

I. L. W. men and I guess they were as hungry as we. At any rate, they got the calf and we got the thrashing. Brentwood raged like a madman the rest of the way home, and he looked like one, what of his torn clothes, swollen nose, and blackened eyes.

There wasn't any more cow-stealing after that. General Folsom sent his troopers out and confiscated all the cows, and his troopers, aided by the militia, ate most of the meat. General Folsom was not to be blamed; it was his duty to maintain law and order, and he maintained it by means of the soldiers, wherefore he was compelled to feed them first of all.

It was about this time that the great panic occurred. The wealthy classes precipitated the flight, and then the slum people caught the contagion and stampeded wildly out of the city. General Folsom was pleased. It was estimated that at least 200,000 had deserted San Francisco, and by that much was his food problem solved. Well do I remember that day. In the morning I had eaten a crust of bread. Half of the afternoon I had stood in the bread line; and after dark I returned home, tired and miserable, carrying a quart of rice and a slice of bacon. Brown met me at the door. His face was worn and terrified. All the servants had fled, he informed me. He alone remained. I was touched by his faithfulness, and when I learned that he had eaten nothing all day, I divided my food with him. We cooked half the rice and half the bacon, sharing it equally and reserving the other half for morning. I went to bed with my hunger, and tossed restlessly all night. In the morning I found Brown had deserted me, and, greater misfortune still, he had stolen what remained of the rice and bacon.

It was a gloomy handful of men that came together at the Club that morning. There was no service at all. The last servant was gone. I noticed, too, that the silver was gone, and I learned where it had gone. The servants had not taken it, for the reason, I presume, that the club members got to it first. Their method of disposing of it was simple.

Down south of Market street, in the dwellings of the I. L. W., the housewives had given square meals in exchange for it. I went back to my house. Yes, my silver was gone all but a massive pitcher. This I wrapped up and carried down south of Market.

I felt better after the meal, and returned to the Club to learn if there was anything new in the situation. Hanover, Collins and Dakon were just leaving. There was no one inside, they told me, and they invited me to come along with them. They were leaving the city, they said, on Dakon's horses, and there was a spare one for me. Dakon had four magnificent carriage horses that he wanted to save, and General Folsom had given him the tip that next morning all the horses that remained in the city were to be confiscated for food. There were not many horses left, for tens of thousands of them had been turned loose into the country when the hay and grain gave out during the first days. Birdall, I remember, who had great draying interests had turned loose 300 dray horses. At an average value of five hundred dollars this had amounted to $150,000. He had hoped, at first, to recover most of the horses after the strike was over, but in the end he never recovered one of them. They were all eaten by the people that fled from San Francisco. For that matter the killing of the army mules and horses for food had already begun.

Fortunately for Dakon, he had had a plentiful supply of hay and grain stored in his stable. We managed to raise four saddles, and we found the animals in good condition and spirited, withal unused to being ridden. I remembered the San Francisco of the Great Earthquake as we rode through the streets, but this San Francisco was vastly more pitiable. No cataclysm of nature had caused this, but rather the tyranny of the labor unions. We rode down past Union Square and through the theatre, hotel and shopping districts. The streets were deserted. Here and there stood automobiles, abandoned where they had broken down or when the gasoline had given out. There was no sign of life, save for the occasional policeman and the soldiers, guarding the banks and public buildings. Once we came upon an I. L. W. man pasting up the latest proclamation. We stopped to read. "We have maintained an orderly strike," it ran; "and we shall maintain order to the end. The end will come when our demands are satisfied, and our demands will be satisfied when we have starved our employers into submission, as we ourselves in the past have often been starved into submission."

"Messener's very words," Collins said. "And I, for one, am ready to submit, only they won't give me a chance to submit. I haven't had a full meal in an age. I wonder what horse-meat tastes like."

We stopped to read another proclamation: "When we think our employers are ready to submit, we shall open up the telegraphs and place the employers' associations of the United States in communication. But only messages relating to peace terms shall be permitted over the wires."

We rode on, crossed Market street, and a little later were passing through the working class districts. Here the streets were not deserted. Leaning over gates or standing in groups, were the I. L. W. men. Happy, well-fed children were playing games, and stout housewives sat on the front steps gossiping. One and all cast amused glances at us. Little children ran after us crying: "Hey, mister, ain't you hungry?" And one woman, a nursing child at her breast, called at Dakon, "Say, Fatty, I will give you a square meal for your skate—ham and potatoes, currant jelly, white bread, canned butter, and two cups of coffee."

"Have you noticed, the last few days," Hanover remarked to me, "that there's not been a stray dog in the streets?"

I had noticed, but I had not thought about it before. It was high time to leave the unfortunate city. We at last managed to connect with the San Bruno Road, along which we headed south. I had a country place near Menlo, and it was our objective. But soon we began to discover that the country was worse off and far more dangerous than the city. There, the soldiers and the I. L. W. kept order; but the country had been turned over to anarchy. Two hundred thousand people had fled south from San Francisco, and we had countless evidences that their flight had been like that of an army of locusts. They had swept everything clean. There had been robbery and fighting. Here and there we passed bodies by the roadside and saw the blackened ruins of farmhouses. The fences were down, and the crops had been trampled by the feet of a multitude. All the vegetable patches had been rooted up by the famished hordes. All the chickens and farm animals had been slaughtered. This was true of all the main roads that led out of San Francisco. Here and there, away from the roads, farmers had held their own with shotguns and revolvers, and were still holding their own. They warned us away and refused to parley with us. And all the destruction and violence had been done by the slum-dwellers and the upper classes. The I. L. W. men, with plentiful food supplies, remained quietly in their homes in the cities.

Early in the day we received concrete proof of how desperate was the situation. To the right of us we heard cries and rifle shots. Bullets whistled dangerously near. There was a crashing in the underbrush; then a magnificent black truck-horse broke across the road in front of us and was gone. We had barely time to notice that he was bleeding and lame. He was followed by three soldiers. The chase went on amongst the trees on the left. We could hear the soldiers calling to one another. A fourth soldier limped out upon the road from the right, sat down on a boulder, and mopped the sweat from his face.

The man grinned up at us and asked for a match. In reply to Dakon's "What's the word?" he informed us that the militiamen were deserting. "No grub," he explained. "They're feedin' it all to the regulars." We also learned from him that the military prisoners had been released from Alcatraz Island because they could no longer be fed.

I shall never forget the next sight we encountered. We

came upon it abruptly, around a turn of the road. Overhead arched the trees. The sunshine was filtering down through the branches. Butterflies were fluttering by, and from the fields came the song of larks. And there stood a powerful touring car. About it and in it lay a number of corpses. It told its own tale. Its occupants, fleeing from the city, had been attacked and dragged down by a gang of slum-dwellers —hoodlums. The thing had occurred within twenty-four hours. Freshly opened meat and fruit tins explained the reason for the attacks. Dakon examined the bodies.

"I thought so," he reported. "I've ridden in that car. It was Periton—the whole family. We've got to watch out for ourselves from now on."

"But we have no food with which to invite attack," I objected.

Dakon pointed to the horse I rode, and I understood.

Early in the day Dakon's horse had cast a shoe. The delicate hoof had split, and by noon the animal was limping. Dakon refused to ride it further, and refused to desert it. So, on his solicitation, we went on. He would lead the horse and join us at my place. That was the last we saw of him; nor did we ever learn his end.

By one o'clock we arrived at the town of Menlo, or rather at the site of Menlo, for it was in ruins. Corpses lay everywhere. The business part of the town, as well as part of the residences, had been gutted by fire. Here and there a residence still held out; but there was no getting near them. When we approached too closely we were fired upon. We met a woman who was poking about in the smoking ruins of her cottage. The first attack, she told us, had been on the stores, and as she talked we could picture that raging, roaring, hungry mob flinging itself upon the handful of townspeople. Millionaires and paupers had fought side by side for the food, and then fought with one another after they got it. The town of Palo Alto and Stanford University had been sacked in similar fashion, we learned. Ahead of us lay a desolate wasted land; and we thought we were wise in turning off to my place. It lay three miles to the west, snuggling among the first rolling swells of the foothills.

But as we rode along we saw that the devastation was not confined to the main roads. The van of the flight had kept to the roads, sacking the small towns as it went; while those that followed had scattered out and swept the whole country-side, like a great broom. My place was built of concrete, masonry, and tiles, and so had escaped being burned, but it was gutted clean. We found the gardener's body in the windmill, littered around with empty shotgun shells. He had put up a good fight. But no trace could be found of the two Italian laborers, nor of the housekeeper and her husband. Not a living thing remained. The calves, the colts, all the fancy poultry and thoroughbred stock, everything was gone. The kitchen and the fireplace where the mob had cooked, were a mess, while many campfires outside bore witness to the large number that had fed and spent the night. What they had not eaten they had carried away. There was not a bite for us.

We spent the rest of the night vainly waiting for Dakon, and in the morning, with our revolvers, fought off half a dozen marauders. Then we killed one of Dakon's horses, hiding for the future what meat we did not immediately eat. In the afternoon Collins went out for a walk, but failed to return. This was the last straw to Hanover. He was for flight there and then, and I had great difficulty in persuading him to wait for daylight. As for myself, I was convinced that the end of the general strike was near, and I was resolved to return to San Francisco. So, in the morning we parted company, Hanover heading south, fifty pounds of horse meat strapped to his saddle, while I, similarly loaded, headed north. Little Hanover pulled through all right, and to the end of his life he will persist, I know, in boring everybody with the narrative of his subsequent adventures.

I got as far as Belmont, on the main road back, when I was robbed of my horse-meat by three militiamen. There was no change in the situation, they said, except that it was going from bad to worse. The I. L. W. had plenty of provisions hidden away and could last out for months. I managed to get as far as Baden, when my horse was taken away from me by a dozen men. Two of them were San Francisco policemen, and the remainder were regular soldiers. This was ominous. The situation was certainly extreme when the regulars were beginning to desert. When I continued my way on foot, they already had the fire started, and the last of Dakon's horses lay slaughtered on the ground.

As luck would have it, I sprained my ankle, and succeeded in getting no further than South San Francisco. I lay there that night in an outhouse, shivering with the cold and at the same time burning with fever. Two days I lay there, too sick to move, and on the third, reeling and giddy, supporting myself on an extemporized crutch I tottered on toward San Francisco. I was weak as well, for it was the third day since food had passed my lips. It was a day of nightmare and torment. As in a dream I passed hundreds of regular soldiers drifting along in the opposite direction, and many policemen, with their families, organized in large groups for mutual protection.

As I entered the city I remembered the workman's house at which I had traded the silver pitcher, and in that direction my hunger drove me. Twilight was falling when I came to the place. I passed around by the alleyway and crawled up the back steps, on which I collapsed. I managed to reach out with the crutch and knocked at the door. Then I must have fainted, for I came to in the kitchen, my face wet with water and whisky being poured down my throat. I choked and spluttered and tried to talk; I began by saying something about not having any more silver pitchers, but that I would make it up to them afterward if they would only give me something to eat. But the housewife interrupted me.

"Why, you poor man!" she said. "Haven't you heard? The strike was called off this afternoon. Of course we'll give you something to eat."

She hustled around, opening a tin of breakfast bacon and preparing to fry it.

"Let me have some now, please," I begged; and I ate the raw bacon on a slice of bread, while her husband explained that the demands of the I. L. W. had been granted. The wires had been opened up in the early afternoon, and everywhere the employers' association had given in. There hadn't been any employers left in San Francisco, but General Folsom had spoken for them. The trains and steamers would start running in the morning, and so would everything else just as soon as system could be established.

And that was the end of the general strike. I never want to see another one. It was worse than a war. A general strike is a cruel and immoral thing, and the brain of man should be capable of running industry in a more rational way. Harrison is still my chauffeur. It was part of the conditions of the I. L. W. that all of its members should be reinstated in their old positions. Brown never came back, but the rest of the servants are with me. I hadn't the heart to discharge them—poor creatures, they were pretty hard pressed when they deserted with the food and silver. And now I can't discharge them. They have all been unionized by the I. L. W. The tyranny of organized labor is getting beyond human endurance. Something must be done.

HOW I BECAME A SOCIALIST

HOW I BECAME A SOCIALIST

It is quite fair to say that I became a Socialist in a fashion somewhat similar to the way in which the Teutonic pagans became Christians—it was hammered into me. Not only was I not looking for Socialism at the time of my conversion, but I was fighting it. I was very young and callow, did not know much of anything, and though I had never even heard of a school called "Individualism," I sang the pæan of the strong with all my heart.

This was because I was strong myself. By strong I mean that I had good health and hard muscles, both of which possessions are easily accounted for. I had lived my childhood on California ranches, my boyhood hustling newspapers on the streets of a healthy Western city, and my youth on the ozone-laden waters of San Francisco Bay and the Pacific Ocean. I loved life in the open, and I toiled in the open, at the hardest kinds of work. Learning no trade, but drifting along from job to job, I looked on the world and called it good, every bit of it. Let me repeat, this optimism was because I was healthy and strong, bothered with neither aches nor weaknesses, never turned down by the boss because I did not look fit, able always to get a job at shovelling coal, sailorizing, or manual labor of some sort.

And because of all this, exulting in my young life, able to hold my own at work or fight, I was a rampant individualist. It was very natural. I was a winner. Wherefore I called the game, as I saw it played, or thought I saw it played, a very proper game for MEN. To be a M A N was to write man in large capitals on my heart. To adventure like a man, and fight like a man, and do a man's work (even for a boy's pay) —these were things that reached right in and gripped hold of

57

me as no other thing could. And I looked ahead into long vistas of a hazy and interminable future, into which, playing what I conceived to be MAN'S game, I should continue to travel with unfailing health, without accidents, and with muscles ever vigorous. As I say, this future was interminable. I could see myself only raging through life without end like one of Nietzsche's *blond beasts,* lustfully roving and conquering by sheer superiority and strength.

As for the unfortunates, the sick, and ailing, and old, and maimed, I must confess I hardly thought of them at all, save that I vaguely felt that they, barring accidents, could be as good as I if they wanted to real hard, and could work just as well. Accidents? Well, they represented FATE, also spelled out in capitals, and there was no getting around FATE. Napoleon had had an accident at Waterloo, but that did not dampen my desire to be another and later Napoleon. Further, the optimism bred of a stomach which could digest scrap iron and a body which flourished on hardships did not permit me to consider accidents as even remotely related to my glorious personality.

I hope I have made it clear that I was proud to be one of Nature's strong-armed noblemen. The dignity of labor was to me the most impressive thing in the world. Without having read Carlyle, or Kipling, I formulated a gospel of work which put theirs in the shade. Work was everything. It was sanctification and salvation. The pride I took in a hard day's work well done would be inconceivable to you. It is almost inconceivable to me as I look back upon it. I was as faithful a wage slave as ever capitalist exploited. To shirk or malinger on the man who paid me my wages was a sin, first, against myself, and second, against him. I considered it a crime second only to treason and just about as bad.

In short, my joyous individualism was dominated by the orthodox bourgeois ethics. I read the bourgeois papers, listened to the bourgeois preachers, and shouted at the sonorous platitudes of the bourgeois politicians. And I doubt not, if other events had not changed my career, that I should have evolved into a professional strike-breaker (one of President Eliot's American heroes), and had my head and my earning power irrevocably smashed by a club in the hands of some militant trades-unionist.

Just about this time, returning from a seven months' voyage before the mast, and just turned eighteen, I took it into my head to go tramping. On rods and blind baggages I fought my way from the open West, where men bucked big and the job hunted the man, to the congested labor centres of the East, where men were small potatoes and hunted the job for all they were worth. And on this new *blond-beast* adventure I found myself looking upon life from a new and totally different angle. I had dropped down from the proletariat into what sociologists love to call the "submerged tenth," and I was startled to discover the way in which that submerged tenth was recruited.

I found there all sorts of men, many of whom had once been as good as myself and just as *blond-beastly*; sailor-men, soldier-men, labor-men, all wrenched and distorted and twisted out of shape by toil and hardship and accident, and cast adrift by their masters like so many old horses. I battered on the drag and slammed back gates with them, or shivered with them in box cars and city parks, listening the while to life-histories which began under auspices as fair as mine, with digestions and bodies equal to and better than mine, and which ended there before my eyes in the shambles at the bottom of the Social Pit.

And as I listened my brain began to work. The woman of the streets and the man of the gutter drew very close to me. I saw the picture of the Social Pit as vividly as though it were a concrete thing, and at the bottom of the Pit I saw them, myself above them, not far, and hanging on the slippery wall by main strength and sweat. And I confess a terror seized me. What when my strength failed? when I should be unable to work shoulder to shoulder with the strong men who were as yet babes unborn? And there and then I swore a great oath. It ran something like this: *All my days I have worked hard with my body, and according to the number of days I have worked, by just that much am I nearer the bottom of the Pit. I shall climb out of the Pit, but not by the muscles of my body shall I climb out. I shall do no more hard work, and may God strike me dead if I do another day's hard work with my body more than I absolutely have to do.* And I have been busy ever since running away from hard work.

Incidentally, while tramping some ten thousand miles through the United States and Canada, I strayed into Niagara Falls, was nabbed by a fee-hunting constable, denied the right to plead guilty or not guilty, sentenced out of hand to thirty days' imprisonment for having no fixed abode and no visible means of support, handcuffed and chained to a bunch of men similarly circumstanced, carted down country to Buffalo, registered at the Erie County Penitentiary, had my head clipped and my budding mustache shaved, was dressed in convict stripes, compulsorily vaccinated by a medical student who practised on such as we, made to march the lock-step, and put to work under the eyes of guards armed with Winchester rifles—all for adventuring in *blond-beastly* fashion. Concerning further details deponent sayeth not, though he may hint that some of his plethoric national patriotism simmered down and leaked out of the bottom of his soul somewhere—at least, since that experience he finds that he cares more for men and women and little children than for imaginary geographical lines.

To return to my conversion. I think it is apparent that my rampant individualism was pretty effectively hammered out of me, and something else as effectively hammered in. But, just as I had been an individualist without knowing it, I was now a Socialist without knowing it, withal, an unscientific one. I had been reborn, but not renamed, and I was running around to find out what manner of thing I was. I ran back to California and opened the books. I do not remember which ones I opened first. It is an unimportant detail anyway. I was already It, whatever It was, and by aid of

the books I discovered that It was a Socialist.   Since that day
I have opened many books, but no economic argument, no
lucid demonstration of the logic and inevitableness of Socialism affects me as profoundly and convincingly as I was af-
fected on the day when I first saw the walls of the Social Pit
rise around me and felt myself slipping down, down, into the
shambles at the bottom.

THE SCAB

THE SCAB

In a competitive society, where men struggle with one another for food and shelter, what is more natural than that generosity, when it diminishes the food and shelter of men other than he who is generous, should be held an accursed thing? Wise old saws to the contrary, he who takes from a man's purse takes from his existence. To strike at a man's food and shelter is to strike at his life; and in a society organized on a tooth-and-nail basis, such an act, performed though it may be under the guise of generosity, is none the less menacing and terrible.

It is for this reason that a laborer is so fiercely hostile to another laborer who offers to work for less pay or longer hours. To hold his place (which is to live), he must offset this offer by another equally liberal, which is equivalent to giving away somewhat from the food and shelter he enjoys. To sell his day's work for $2, instead of $2.50, means that he, his wife, and his children will not have so good a roof over their heads, so warm clothes on their backs, so substantial food in their stomachs. Meat will be bought less frequently and it will be tougher and less nutritious, stout new shoes will go less often on the children's feet, and disease and death will be more imminent in a cheaper house and neighborhood.

Thus the generous laborer, giving more of a day's work for less return (measured in terms of food and shelter), threatens the life of his less generous brother laborer, and at the best, if he does not destroy that life, he diminishes it. Whereupon the less generous laborer looks upon him as an enemy, and, as men are inclined to do in a tooth-and-nail society, he tries to kill the man who is trying to kill him.

When a striker kills with a brick the man who has taken his place, he has no sense of wrong-doing. In the deepest

65

holds of his being, though he does not reason the impulse, he has an ethical sanction.   He feels dimly that he has justification, such as the home-defending Boer felt (though more sharply), with each bullet he fired at the invading English. Behind every brick thrown by a striker is the selfish will "to live" of himself, and the slightly altruistic will "to live" of his family.   The family group came into the world before the State group, and society, being still on the primitive basis of tooth and nail, the will "to live" of the State is not so compelling to the striker as is the will "to live" of his family and himself.

In addition to the use of bricks, clubs, and bullets, the selfish laborer finds it necessary to express his feelings in speech.   Just as the peaceful country-dweller calls the sea-rover a "pirate," and the stout burgher calls the man who breaks into his strongbox a "robber," so the selfish laborer applies the opprobrious epithet "scab" to the laborer who takes from him food and shelter by being more generous in the disposal of his labor power.   The sentimental connotation of "scab" is as terrific as that of "traitor" or "Judas," and a sentimental definition would be as deep and varied as the human heart.   It is far easier to arrive at what may be called a technical definition, worded in commercial terms, as, for instance, that *a scab is one who gives more value for the same price than another.*

The laborer who gives more time or strength or skill for the same wage than another, or equal time or strength or skill for a less wage, is a scab.   This generousness on his part is hurtful to his fellow-laborers, for it compels them to an equal generousness which is not to their liking, and which gives them less of food and shelter.   But a word may be said for the scab.   Just as his act makes his rivals compulsorily generous, so do they, by fortune of birth and training, make compulsory his act of generousness.   He does not scab because he wants to scab.   No whim of the spirit, no burgeoning of the heart, leads him to give more of his labor power than they for a certain sum.

It is because he cannot get work on the same terms as they that he is a scab. There is less work than there are men to do work. This is patent, else the scab would not loom so large on the labor-market horizon. Because they are stronger than he, or more skilled, or more energetic, it is impossible for him to take their places at the same wage. To take their places he must give more value, must work longer hours or receive a smaller wage. He does so, and he cannot help it, for his will "to live" is driving him on as well as they are being driven on by their will "to live"; and to live he must win food and shelter, which he can do only by receiving permission to work from some man who owns a bit of land or a piece of machinery. And to receive permission from this man, he must make the transaction profitable for him.

Viewed in this light, the scab, who gives more labor power for a certain price than his fellows, is not so generous after all. He is no more generous with his energy than the chattel slave and the convict laborer, who, by the way, are the almost perfect scabs. They give their labor power for about the minimum possible price. But, within limits, they may loaf and malinger, and, as scabs, are exceeded by the machine, which never loafs and malingers and which is the ideally perfect scab.

It is not nice to be a scab. Not only is it not in good social taste and comradeship but, from the standpoint of food and shelter, it is bad business policy. Nobody desires to scab, to give most for least. The ambition of every individual is quite the opposite, to give least for most; and, as a result, living in a tooth-and-nail society, battle royal is waged by the ambitious individuals. But in its most salient aspect, that of the struggle over the division of the joint product, it is no longer a battle between individuals, but between groups of individuals. Capital and labor apply themselves to raw material, make something useful out of it, add to its value, and then proceed to quarrel over the division of the added value. Neither cares to give most for least. Each is intent on giving less than the other and on receiving more.

Labor combines into its unions, capital into partnerships, associations, corporations, and trusts. A group-struggle is the result, in which the individuals, as individuals, play no part. The Brotherhood of Carpenters and Joiners, for instance, serves notice on the Master Builders' Association that it demands an increase of the wage of its members from $3.50 a day to $4, and a Saturday half-holiday without pay. This means that the carpenters are trying to give less for more. Where they received $21 for six full days, they are endeavoring to get $22 for five days and a half,—that is, they will work half a day less each week and receive a dollar more.

Also, they expect the Saturday half-holiday to give work to one additional man for each eleven previously employed. This last affords a splendid example of the development of the group idea. In this particular struggle the individual has no chance at all for life. The individual carpenter would be crushed like a mote by the Master Builders' Association, and like a mote the individual master builder would be crushed by the Brotherhood of Carpenters and Joiners.

In the group-struggle over the division of the joint product, labor utilizes the union with its two great weapons, the strike and the boycott; while capital utilizes the trust and the association, the weapons of which are the black-list, the lockout, and the scab. The scab is by far the most formidable weapon of the three. He is the man who breaks strikes and causes all the trouble. Without him there would be no trouble, for the strikers are willing to remain out peacefully and indefinitely so long as other men are not in their places, and so long as the particular aggregation of capital with which they are fighting is eating its head off in enforced idleness.

But both warring groups have reserve weapons. Were it not for the scab, these weapons would not be brought into play. But the scab takes the place of the striker, who begins at once to wield a most powerful weapon, terrorism. The will "to live" of the scab recoils from the menace of broken bones and violent death. With all due respect to the labor leaders, who are not to be blamed for volubly asseverating otherwise, terrorism is a well-defined and eminently successful policy of the labor unions. It has probably won them more strikes than all the rest of the weapons in their arsenal. This terrorism, however, must be clearly understood. It is directed solely against the scab, placing him in such fear for life and limb as to drive him out of the contest. But when terrorism gets out of hand and inoffensive non-combatants are injured, law and order threatened, and property destroyed, it becomes an edged tool that cuts both ways. This sort of terrorism is sincerely deplored by the labor leaders, for it has probably lost them as many strikes as have been lost by any other single cause.

The scab is powerless under terrorism. As a rule, he is not so good nor gritty a man as the men he is displacing, and he lacks their fighting organization. He stands in dire need of stiffening and backing. His employers, the capitalists, draw their two remaining weapons, the ownership of which is debatable, but which they for the time being happen to control. These two weapons may be called the political and judicial machinery of society. When the scab crumples up and is ready to go down before the fists, bricks, and bullets of the labor group, the capitalist group puts the police and soldiers into the field, and begins a general bombardment of injunctions. Victory usually follows, for the labor group cannot withstand the combined assault of Gatling guns and injunctions.

But it has been noted that the ownership of the political and judicial machinery of society is debatable. In the Titanic struggle over the division of the joint product, each group reaches out for every available weapon. Nor are they blinded by the smoke of conflict. They fight their battles as coolly and collectedly as ever battles were fought on paper. The capitalist group has long since realized the immense importance of controlling the political and judicial machinery of society. Taught by Gatlings and injunctions, which have smashed many an otherwise successful strike, the labor group is beginning to realize that it all depends upon who is behind and who is before the Gatlings and the injunctions. And he who knows the labor movement knows that there is slowly growing up and being formulated a clear and definite policy for the capture of the political and judicial machinery.

This is the terrible spectre which Mr. John Graham Brooks sees looming portentously over the twentieth century world. No man may boast a more intimate knowledge of the labor movement than he; and he reiterates again and again the dangerous likelihood of the whole labor group capturing the political machinery of society. As he says in his recent book:[1] "It is not probable that employers can destroy unionism in the United States. Adroit and desperate attempts will, however, be made, if we mean by unionism the undisciplined and aggressive fact of vigorous and determined organizations. If capital should prove too strong in this struggle, the result is easy to predict. The employers have only to convince organized labor that it cannot hold its own against the capitalist manager, and the whole energy that now goes to the union will turn to an aggressive political socialism. It will not be the harmless sympathy with increased city and state functions which trade unions already feel; it will become a turbulent political force bent upon using every weapon of taxation against the rich."

This struggle not to be a scab, to avoid giving more for less and to succeed in giving less for more, is more vital than it would appear on the surface. The capitalist and labor groups are locked together in desperate battle, and neither side is swayed by moral considerations more than skin-deep. The labor group hires business agents, lawyers, and organizers, and is beginning to intimidate legislators by the strength of its solid vote; and more directly, in the near future, it will attempt to control legislation by capturing it bodily through the ballot-box. On the other hand, the capitalist group, numerically weaker, hires newspapers, universities, and legislatures, and strives to bend to its need all the forces which go to mould public opinion.

---

[1] *The Social Unrest.* Macmillan Company.

The only honest morality displayed by either side is white-hot indignation at the iniquities of the other side. The striking teamster complacently takes a scab driver into an alley, and with an iron bar breaks his arms, so that he can drive no more, but cries out to high Heaven for justice when the capitalist breaks his skull by means of a club in the hands of a policeman. Nay, the members of a union will declaim in impassioned rhetoric for the God-given right of an eight-hour day, and at the time be working their own business agent seventeen hours out of the twenty-four.

A capitalist such as Collis P. Huntington, and his name is legion, after a long life spent in buying the aid of countless legislatures, will wax virtuously wrathful, and condemn in unmeasured terms "the dangerous tendency of crying out to the Government for aid" in the way of labor legislation. Without a quiver, a member of the capitalist group will run tens of thousands of pitiful child-laborers through his life-destroying cotton factories, and weep maudlin and constitutional tears over one scab hit in the back with a brick. He will drive a "compulsory" free contract with an unorganized laborer on the basis of a starvation wage, saying, "Take it or leave it," knowing that to leave it means to die of hunger, and in the next breath, when the organizer entices that laborer into a union, will storm patriotically about the inalienable right of all men to work. In short, the chief moral concern of either side is with the morals of the other side. They are not in the business for their moral welfare, but to achieve the enviable position of the non-scab who gets more than he gives.

But there is more to the question than has yet been discussed. The labor scab is no more detestable to his brother laborers than is the capitalist scab to his brother capitalists. A capitalist may get most for least in dealing with his laborers, and in so far be a non-scab; but at the same time, in his dealings with his fellow-capitalists, he may give most for least and be the very worst kind of scab. The most heinous crime an employer of labor can commit is to scab on his fellow-employers of labor. Just as the individual laborers have

organized into groups to protect themselves from the peril of
the scab laborer, so have the employers organized into groups
to protect themselves from the peril of the scab employer.
The employers' federations, associations, and trusts are nothing
more nor less than unions. They are organized to destroy
scabbing amongst themselves and to encourage scabbing
amongst others. For this reason they pool interests, determine
prices, and present an unbroken and aggressive front to the
labor group.

As has been said before, nobody likes to play the compulsorily generous role of scab. It is a bad business proposition
on the face of it. And it is patent that there would be no
capitalist scabs if there were not more capital than there is
work for capital to do. When there are enough factories in
existence to supply, with occasional stoppages, a certain commodity, the building of new factories by a rival concern, for
the production of that commodity, is plain advertisement that
that capital is out of a job. The first act of this new aggregation of capital will be to cut prices, to give more for less,—
in short to scab, to strike at the very existence of the less
generous aggregation of capital the work of which it is trying
to do.

No scab capitalist strives to give more for less for any other
reason than that he hopes, by undercutting a competitor and
driving that competitor out of the market, to get that market
and its profits for himself. His ambition is to achieve the
day when he shall stand alone in the field both as buyer and
seller,—when he will be the royal non-scab, buying most for
least, selling least for most, and reducing all about him, the
small buyers and sellers (the consumers and the laborers), to
a general condition of scabdom. This, for example, has been
the history of Mr. Rockefeller and the Standard Oil Company.
Through all the sordid villainies of scabdom he has passed,
until today he is a most regal non-scab. However, to continue in this enviable position, he must be prepared at a
moment's notice to go scabbing again. And he is prepared.
Whenever a competitor arises, Mr. Rockefeller changes about

from giving least for most and gives most for least with such a vengeance as to drive the competitor out of existence.

The banded capitalists discriminate against a scab capitalist by refusing him trade advantages, and by combining against him in most relentless fashion. The banded laborers, discriminating against a scab laborer in more primitive fashion, with a club, are no more merciless than the banded capitalists.

Mr. Casson tells of a New York capitalist who withdrew from the Sugar Union several years ago and became a scab. He was worth something like twenty millions of dollars. But the Sugar Union, standing shoulder to shoulder with the Railroad Union and several other unions, beat him to his knees till he cried "Enough." So frightfully did they beat him that he was obliged to turn over to his creditors his home, his chickens, and his gold watch. In point of fact, he was as thoroughly bludgeoned by the Federation of Capitalist Unions as ever scab workman was bludgeoned by a labor union. The intent in either case is the same,—to destroy the scab's producing power. The labor scab with concussion of the brain is put out of business, and so is the capitalist scab who has lost all his dollars down to his chickens and his watch.

But the role of scab passes beyond the individual. Just as individuals scab on other individuals, so do groups scab on other groups. And the principle involved is precisely the same as in the case of the simple labor scab. A group, in the nature of its organization, is often compelled to give most for least, and so doing, to strike at the life of another group. At the present moment all Europe is appalled by that colossal scab, the United States. And Europe is clamorous with agitation for a Federation of National Unions to protect her from the United States. It may be remarked, in passing, that in its prime essentials this agitation in no wise differs from the trade-union agitation among workmen in any industry. The trouble is caused by the scab who is giving most for least. The result of the American scab's nefarious actions will be to strike at the food and shelter of Europe. The way for Europe to protect herself is to quit bickering among her parts and to form a union against the scab. And if the union is formed, armies and navies may be expected to be brought into play in fashion similar to the bricks and clubs in ordinary labor struggles.

In this connection, and as one of many walking delegates for the nations, M. Leroy-Beaulieu, the noted French economist, may well be quoted. In a letter to the Vienna *Tageblatt*, he advocates an economic alliance among the Continental nations for the purpose of barring out American goods, an economic alliance, in his own language, *"which may possibly and desirably develop into a political alliance."*

It will be noted, in the utterances of the Continental walking delegates, that, one and all, they leave England out of the proposed union. And in England herself the feeling is growing that her days are numbered if she cannot unite for offence and defence with the great American scab. As Andrew Carnegie said some time ago, "The only course for Great Britain seems to be reunion with her grandchild or sure decline to a secondary place, and then to comparative insignificance in the future annals of the English-speaking race."

Cecil Rhodes, speaking of what would have obtained but for the pig-headedness of George III, and of what will obtain when England and the United States are united, said, "No cannon would . . . be fired on either hemisphere but by permission of the English race." It would seem that England, fronted by the hostile Continental Union and flanked by the great American scab, has nothing left but to join with the scab and play the historic labor role of armed Pinkerton. Granting the words of Cecil Rhodes, the United States would be enabled to scab without let or hindrance on Europe, while England, as professional strike-breaker and policeman, destroyed the unions and kept order.

All this may appear fantastic and erroneous, but there is in it a soul of truth vastly more significant than it may seem. Civilization may be expressed today in terms of trade-unionism. Individual struggles have largely passed away, but group-struggles increase prodigiously. And the things for which the groups struggle are the same as of old. Shorn of all subtleties and complexities, the chief struggle of men, and of groups of men, is for food and shelter. And, as of old they struggled with tooth and nail, so today they struggle with teeth and nails elongated into armies and navies, machines, and economic advantages.

Under the definition that a scab is *one who gives more value for the same price than another,* it would seem that society can be generally divided into the two classes of the scabs and the non-scabs. But on closer investigation, however, it will be seen that the non-scab is a vanishing quantity. In the social jungle, everybody is preying upon everybody else. As in the case of Mr. Rockefeller, he who was a scab yesterday is a non-scab today, and tomorrow may be a scab again.

The woman stenographer or bookkeeper who receives forty dollars per month where a man was receiving seventy-five is a scab. So is the woman who does a man's work at a weaving-machine, and the child who goes into the mill or factory. And the father, who is scabbed out of work by the wives and children of other men, sends his own wife and children to scab in order to save himself.

When a publisher offers an author better royalties than other publishers have been paying him, he is scabbing on those other publishers. The reporter on a newspaper, who feels he should be receiving a larger salary for his work, says so, and is shown the door, is replaced by a reporter who is a scab; whereupon, when the belly-need presses, the displaced reporter goes to another paper and scabs himself. The minister who hardens his heart to a call, and waits for a certain congregation to offer him say $500 a year more, often finds himself scabbed upon by another and more impecunious minister; and the next time it is *his* turn to scab while a brother minister is hardening his heart to a call. The scab is everywhere. The professional strike-breakers, who as a class receive large wages, will scab on one another, while scab unions are even formed to prevent scabbing upon scabs.

There are non-scabs, but they are usually born so, and are protected by the whole might of society in the possession of their food and shelter. King Edward is such a type, as are all individuals who receive hereditary food-and-shelter privileges,—such as the present Duke of Bedford, for instance, who yearly receives $75,000 from the good people of London because some former king gave some former ancestor of his the market privileges of Covent Garden. The irresponsible rich are likewise non-scabs,—and by them is meant that coupon-clipping class which hires its managers and brains to invest the money usually left it by its ancestors.

Outside these lucky creatures, all the rest, at one time or another in their lives, are scabs, at one time or another are engaged in giving more for a certain price than any one else. The meek professor in some endowed institution, by his meek suppression of his convictions, is giving more for his salary than gave the other and more outspoken professor whose chair he occupies. And when a political party dangles a full dinner-pail in the eyes of the toiling masses, it is offering more for a vote than the dubious dollar of the opposing party. Even a money-lender is not above taking a slightly lower rate of interest and saying nothing about it.

Such is the tangle of conflicting interests in a tooth-and-nail society that people cannot avoid being scabs, are often made so against their desires, and are often unconsciously made so. When several trades in a certain locality demand and receive an advance in wages, they are unwittingly making scabs of their fellow-labourers in that district who have received no advance in wages. In San Francisco the barbers, laundry-workers, and milk-wagon drivers received such an advance in wages. Their employers promptly ˙added the amount of this advance to the selling price of their wares. The price of shaves, of washing, and of milk went up. This reduced the purchasing power of the unorganized laborers, and, in point of fact, reduced their wages and made them greater scabs.

Because the British laborer is disinclined to scab,—that is, because he restricts his output in order to give less for the wage he receives,—it is to a certain extent made possible for the American capitalist, who receives a less restricted output from his laborers, to play the scab on the English capitalist. As a result of this (of course combined with other causes), the American capitalist and the American laborer are striking at the food and shelter of the English capitalist and laborer.

The English laborer is starving today because, among other things, he is not a scab. He practises the policy of "ca' canny," which may be defined as "go easy." In order to get most for least, in many trades he performs but from one-fourth to one-sixth of the labor he is well able to perform. An instance of this is found in the building of the Westinghouse Electric Works at Manchester. The British limit per man was 400 bricks per day. The Westinghouse Company imported a "driving" American contractor, aided by half a dozen "driving" American foremen, and the British brick-layer swiftly attained an average of 1800 bricks per day, with a maximum of 2500 bricks for the plainest work.

But the British laborer's policy of "ca' canny," which is the very honorable one of giving least for most, and which is likewise the policy of the English capitalist, is nevertheless frowned upon by the English capitalist, whose business existence is threatened by the great American scab. From the rise of the factory system, the English capitalist gladly embraced the opportunity, wherever he found it, of giving least for most. He did it all over the world whenever he enjoyed a market monopoly, and he did it at home with the laborers employed in his mills, destroying them like flies till prevented, within limits, by the passage of the Factory Acts. Some of the proudest fortunes of England today may trace their origin to the giving of least for most to the miserable slaves of the factory towns. But at the present time the English capitalist is outraged because his laborers are employing against him precisely the same policy he employed against them, and which he would employ again did the chance present itself.

Yet "ca' canny" is a disastrous thing to the British laborer. It has driven shipbuilding from England to Scotland, bottle-making from Scotland to Belgium, flint-glass-making from England to Germany, and today is steadily driving industry after industry to other countries. A correspondent from Northampton wrote not long ago: "Factories are working half and third time. . . . There is no strike, there is no real labor trouble, but the masters and men are alike suffering from sheer lack of employment. Markets which were once theirs are now American." It would seem that the unfortunate British laborer is 'twixt the devil and the deep sea. If he gives most for least, he faces a frightful slavery such as marked the beginning of the factory system. If he gives least for most, he drives industry away to other countries and has no work at all.

But the union laborers of the United States have nothing of which to boast, while, according to their trade-union ethics, they have a great deal of which to be ashamed. They passionately preach short hours and big wages, the shorter the hours and the bigger the wages the better. Their hatred for a scab is as terrible as the hatred of a patriot for a traitor, of a Christian for a Judas. And in the face of all this, they are as colossal scabs as the United States is a colossal scab. For all their boasted unions and high labor ideals, they are about the most thorough-going scabs on the planet.

Receiving $4.50 per day, because of his proficiency and immense working power, the American laborer has been known to scab upon scabs (so called) who took his place and received only $0.90 per day for a longer day. In this particular instance, five Chinese coolies, working longer hours, gave less value for the price received from their employer than did one American laborer.

It is upon his brother laborers overseas that the American laborer most outrageously scabs. As Mr. Casson has shown, an English nail-maker gets $3 per week, while an American nail-maker gets $30. But the English worker turns out 200 pounds of nails per week, while the American turns out 5500 pounds. If he were as "fair" as his English brother, other things being equal, he would be receiving, at the English worker's rate of pay, $82.50. As it is, he is scabbing upon his English brother to the tune of $52.50 per week. Dr. Schultze-Gaevernitz has shown that a German weaver produces 466 yards of cotton a week at a cost of .303 per yard, while an American weaver produces 1200 yards at a cost of .02 per yard.

But, it may be objected, a great part of this is due to the more improved American machinery. Very true, but none the less a great part is still due to the superior energy, skill, and willingness of the American laborer. The English laborer is faithful to the policy of "ca' canny." He refuses point-blank to get the work out of a machine that the New World scab gets out of a machine. Mr. Maxim, observing a wasteful hand-labor process in his English factory, invented a machine which he proved capable of displacing several men. But workman after workman was put at the machine, and without exception they turned out neither more nor less than a workman turned out by hand. They obeyed the mandate of the union and went easy, while Mr. Maxim gave up in despair. Nor will the British workman run machines at as high speed as the American, nor will he run so many. An American workman will "give equal attention simultaneously to three, four, or six machines or tools, while the British workman is compelled by his trade union to limit his attention to one, so that employment may be given to half a dozen men."

But, for scabbing, no blame attaches itself anywhere. With rare exceptions, all the people in the world are scabs. The strong, capable workman gets a job and holds it because of his strength and capacity. And he holds it because out of his strength and capacity he gives a better value for his wage than does the weaker and less capable workman. Therefore he is scabbing upon his weaker and less capable brother workman. He is giving more value for the price paid by the employer.

The superior workman scabs upon the inferior workman because he is so constituted and cannot help it. The one, by fortune of birth and upbringing, is strong and capable; the other, by fortune of birth and upbringing, is not so strong nor capable. It is for the same reason that one country scabs upon another. That country which has the good fortune to possess great natural resources, a finer sun and soil, unhampering institutions, and a deft and intelligent labor class and capitalist class is bound to scab upon a country less fortunately situated. It is the good fortune of the United States that is making her the colossal scab, just as it is the good fortune of one man to be born with a straight back while his brother is born with a hump.

It is not good to give most for least, not good to be a scab. The word has gained universal opprobrium. On the other hand, to be a non-scab, to give least for most, is universally branded as stingy, selfish, and unchristian-like. So all the world, like the British workman, is 'twixt the devil and the deep sea. It is treason to one's fellows to scab, it is unchristian-like not to scab.

Since to give least for most, and to give most for least, are universally bad, what remains? Equity remains, which is to give like for like, the same for the same, neither more nor less. But this equity, society, as at present constituted, cannot give. It is not in the nature of present-day society for men to give like for like, the same for the same. And so long as men continue to live in this competitive society, struggling tooth and nail with one another for food and shelter (which is to struggle tooth and nail with one another for life), that long will the scab continue to exist. His will "to live" will force him to exist. He may be flouted and jeered by his brothers, he may be beaten with bricks and clubs by the men who by superior strength and capacity scab upon him as he scabs upon them by longer hours and smaller wages, but through it all he will persist, giving a bit more of most for least than they are giving.

January, 1904.

WHAT LIFE MEANS TO ME

WHAT LIFE MEANS TO ME

I WAS born in the working-class. Early I discovered enthusiasm, ambition, and ideals; and to satisfy these became the problem of my child-life. My environment was crude and rough and raw. I had no outlook, but an uplook rather. My place in society was at the bottom. Here life offered nothing but sordidness and wretchedness, both of the flesh and the spirit; for here flesh and spirit were alike starved and tormented.

Above me towered the colossal edifice of society, and to my mind the only way out was up. Into this edifice I early resolved to climb. Up above, men wore black clothes and boiled shirts, and women dressed in beautiful gowns. Also, there were good things to eat, and there was plenty to eat. This much for the flesh. Then there were the things of the spirit. Up above me, I knew, were unselfishnesses of the spirit, clean and noble thinking, keen intellectual living. I knew all this because I read "Seaside Library" novels, in which, with the exception of the villians and adventuresses, all men and women thought beautiful thoughts, spoke a beautiful tongue, and performed glorious deeds. In short, as I accepted the rising of the sun, I accepted that up above me was all that was fine and noble and gracious, all that gave decency and dignity to life, all that made life worth living and that remunerated one for his travail and misery.

But it is not particularly easy for one to climb up out of the working-class—especially if he is handicapped by the possession of ideals and illusions. I lived on a ranch in California, and I was hard put to find the ladder whereby to climb. I early inquired the rate of interest on invested money, and worried my child's brain into an understanding of the virtues and excellencies of that remarkable invention of man, compound interest. Further, I ascertained the current rates of wages for workers of all ages, and the cost of living. From all this data I concluded that if I began immediately and worked and saved until I was fifty years of age, I could then stop working and enter into participation in a fair portion of the delights and goodnesses that would then be open to me higher up in society. Of course, I resolutely determined not to marry, while I quite forgot to consider at all that great rock of disaster in the working-class world —sickness.

But the life that was in me demanded more than a meagre existence of scraping and scrimping. Also, at ten years of age, I became a newsboy on the streets of a city, and found myself with a changed uplook. All about me were still the same sordidness and wretchedness, and up above me was still the same paradise waiting to be gained; but the ladder whereby to climb was a different one. It was now the ladder of business. Why save my earnings and invest in government bonds, when, by buying two newspapers for five cents, with a turn of the wrist I could sell them for ten cents and double my capital? The business ladder was the ladder for me, and I had a vision of myself becoming a baldheaded and successful merchant prince.

Alas for visions! When I was sixteen I had already earned the title of "prince." But this title was given me by a gang of cut-throats and thieves, by whom I was called "The Prince of the Oyster Pirates." And at that time I had climbed the first rung of the business ladder. I was a capitalist. I owned a boat and a complete oyster-pirating outfit. I had begun to exploit my fellow-creatures. I had a crew of one man. As captain and owner I took two-thirds of the spoils, and gave the crew one-third, though the crew worked just as hard as I did and risked just as much his life and liberty.

This one rung was the height I climbed up the business ladder. One night I went on a raid amongst the Chinese

fishermen. Ropes and nets were worth dollars and cents. It
was robbery, I grant, but it was precisely the spirit of capitalism. The capitalist takes away the possessions of his fellow-
creatures by means of a rebate, or of a betrayal of trust, or
by the purchase of senators and supreme-court judges. I was
merely crude. That was the only difference. I used a gun.

But my crew that night was one of those inefficients
against whom the capitalist is wont to fulminate, because,
forsooth, such inefficients increase expenses and reduce dividends. My crew did both. What of his carelessness he set
fire to the big mainsail and totally destroyed it. There weren't
any dividends that night, and the Chinese fishermen were
richer by the nets and ropes we did not get. I was bankrupt, unable just then to pay sixty-five dollars for a new
mainsail. I left my boat at anchor and went off on a bay-
pirate boat on a raid up the Sacramento River. While away
on this trip, another gang of bay pirates raided my boat.
They stole everything, even the anchors; and later on, when
I recovered the drifting hulk, I sold it for twenty dollars.
I had slipped back the one rung I had climbed, and never
again did I attempt the business ladder.

From then on I was mercilessly exploited by other capitalists.
I had the muscle, and they made money out of it while I
made but a very indifferent living out of it. I was a sailor
before the mast, a longshoreman, a roustabout; I worked in
canneries, and factories, and laundries; I mowed lawns, and
cleaned carpets, and washed windows. And I never got the
full product of my toil. I looked at the daughter of the
cannery owner, in her carriage, and knew that it was my
muscle, in part, that helped drag along that carriage on its
rubber tires. I looked at the son of the factory owner, going
to college, and knew that it was my muscle that helped, in
part, to pay for the wine and good fellowship he enjoyed.

But I did not resent this. It was all in the game. They
were the strong. Very well, I was strong. I would carve
my way to a place amongst them and make money out of

the muscles of other men. I was not afraid of work. I loved hard work. I would pitch in and work harder than ever and eventually become a pillar of society.

And just then, as luck would have it, I found an employer that was of the same mind. I was willing to work, and he was more than willing that I should work. I thought I was learning a trade. In reality, I had displaced two men. I thought he was making an electrician out of me; as a matter of fact, he was making fifty dollars per month out of me. The two men I had displaced had received forty dollars each per month; I was doing the work of both for thirty dollars per month.

This employer worked me nearly to death. A man may love oysters, but too many oysters will disincline him toward that particular diet. And so with me. Too much work sickened me. I did not wish ever to see work again. I fled from work. I became a tramp, begging my way from door to door, wandering over the United States and sweating bloody sweats in slums and prisons.

I had been born in the working-class, and I was now, at the age of eighteen, beneath the point at which I had started. I was down in the cellar of society, down in the subterranean depths of misery about which it is neither nice nor proper to speak. I was in the pit, the abyss, the human cesspool, the shambles and charnel-house of our civilization. This is the part of the edifice of society that society chooses to ignore. Lack of space compels me here to ignore it, and I shall say only that the things I there saw gave me a terrible scare.

I was scared into thinking. I saw the naked simplicities of the complicated civilization in which I lived. Life was a matter of food and shelter. In order to get food and shelter men sold things. The merchant sold shoes, the politician sold his manhood, and the representative of the people, with exceptions, of course, sold his trust; while nearly all sold their honor. Women, too, whether on the street or in the holy bond of wedlock, were prone to sell their flesh. All things were commodities, all people bought and sold. The one commodity that labor had to sell was muscle. The honor of labor had no price in the market-place. Labor had muscle, and muscle alone, to sell.

But there was a difference, a vital difference. Shoes and trust and honor had a way of renewing themselves. They were imperishable stocks. Muscle, on the other hand, did not renew. As the shoe merchant sold shoes, he continued to replenish his stock. But there was no way of replenishing the laborer's stock of muscle. The more he sold of his muscle, the less of it remained to him. It was his one commodity, and each day his stock of it diminished. In the end, if he did not die before, he sold out and put up his shutters. He was a muscle bankrupt, and nothing remained to him but to go down into the cellar of society and perish miserably.

I learned, further, that brain was likewise a commodity. It, too, was different from muscle. A brain seller was only at his prime when he was fifty or sixty years old, and his wares were fetching higher prices than ever. But a laborer was worked out or broken down at forty-five or fifty. I had been in the cellar of society, and I did not like the place as a habitation. The pipes and drains were unsanitary, and the air was bad to breathe. If I could not live on the parlor floor of society, I could, at any rate, have a try at the attic. It was true, the diet there was slim, but the air at least was pure. So I resolved to sell no more muscle, and to become a vender of brains.

Then began a frantic pursuit of knowledge. I returned to California and opened the books. While thus equipping myself to become a brain merchant, it was inevitable that I should delve into sociology. There I found, in a certain class of books, scientifically formulated, the simple sociological concepts I had already worked out for myself. Other and greater minds, before I was born, had worked out all that I had thought and a vast deal more. I discovered that I was a socialist.

The socialists were revolutionists, inasmuch as they struggled to overthrow the society of the present, and out of the material to build the society of the future. I, too, was a socialist and a revolutionist. I joined the groups of working-class and intellectual revolutionists, and for the first time came into intellectual living. Here I found keen-flashing intellects and brilliant wits; for here I met strong and alert-brained, withal horny-handed, members of the working-class; unfrocked preachers too wide in their Christianity for any congregation of Mammon-worshippers; professors broken on the wheel of university subservience to the ruling class and flung out because they were quick with knowledge which they strove to apply to the affairs of mankind.

Here I found, also, warm faith in the human, glowing idealism, sweetnesses of unselfishness, renunciation, and martyrdom—all the splendid, stinging things of the spirit. Here life was clean, noble, and alive. Here life rehabilitated itself, became wonderful and glorious; and I was glad to be alive. I was in touch with great souls who exalted flesh and spirit over dollars and cents, and to whom the thin wail of the starved slum child meant more than all the pomp and circumstance of commercial expansion and world empire. All about me were nobleness of purpose and heroism of effort, and my days and nights were sunshine and starshine, all fire and dew, with before my eyes, ever burning and blazing, the Holy Grail, Christ's own Grail, the warm human, long-suffering and maltreated, but to be rescued and saved at the last.

And I, poor foolish I, deemed all this to be a mere foretaste of the delights of living I should find higher above me in society. I had lost many illusions since the day I read "Sea-side Library" novels on the California ranch. I was destined to lose many of the illusions I still retained.

As a brain merchant I was a success. Society opened its portals to me. I entered right in on the parlor floor, and my disillusionment proceeded rapidly. I sat down to dinner with the masters of society, and with the wives and daughters of the masters of society. The women were gowned beautifully, I admit; but to my naïve surprise I discovered that they were of the same clay as all the rest of the women I had known down below in the cellar. "The colonel's lady and Judy O'Grady were sisters under their skins"—and gowns.

It was not this, however, so much as their materialism, that shocked me. It is true, these beautifully gowned, beautiful women prattled sweet little ideals and dear little moralities; but in spite of their prattle the dominant key of the life they lived was materialistic. And they were so sentimentally selfish! They assisted in all kinds of sweet little charities, and informed one of the fact, while all the time the food they ate and the beautiful clothes they wore were bought out of dividends stained with the blood of child labor, and sweated labor, and of prostitution itself. When I mentioned such facts, expecting in my innocence that these sisters of Judy O'Grady would at once strip off their blood-dyed silks and jewels, they became excited and angry, and read me preachments about the lack of thrift, the drink, and the innate depravity that caused all the misery in society's cellar. When I mentioned that I couldn't quite see that it was the lack of thrift, the intemperance, and the depravity of a half-starved child of six that made it work twelve hours every night in a Southern cotton mill, these sisters of Judy O'Grady attacked my private life and called me an "agitator"—as though that, forsooth, settled the argument.

Nor did I fare better with the masters themselves. I had expected to find men who were clean, noble, and alive, whose ideals were clean, noble, and alive. I went about amongst the men who sat in the high places—the preachers, the politicians, the business men, the professors, and the editors. I ate meat with them, drank wine with them, automobiled with them, and studied them. It is true, I found many that were clean and noble; but with rare exceptions, they were not *alive*. I do verily believe I could count the exceptions on the fingers of my two hands. Where they were not alive with rottenness, quick with unclean life, they were merely the unburied dead—clean and noble, like well-preserved mummies, but not alive. In this connection I may especially mention the professors I met, the men who live up to that decadent university ideal, "the passionless pursuit of passionless intelligence."

I met men who invoked the name of the Prince of Peace in their diatribes against war, and who put rifles in the hands of Pinkertons with which to shoot down strikers in their own factories. I met men incoherent with indignation at the brutality of prize-fighting, and who, at the same time, were parties to the adulteration of food that killed each year more babies than even red-handed Herod had killed.

I talked in hotels and clubs and homes and Pullmans and steamer-chairs with captains of industry, and marvelled at how little travelled they were in the realm of intellect. On the other hand, I discovered that their intellect, in the business sense, was abnormally developed. Also, I discovered that their morality, where business was concerned, was nil.

This delicate, aristocratic-featured gentleman, was a dummy director and a tool of corporations that secretly robbed widows and orphans. This gentleman, who collected fine editions and was an especial patron of literature, paid blackmail to a heavy-jowled, black-browed boss of a municipal machine. This editor, who published patent medicine advertisements and did not dare print the truth in his paper about said patent medicines for fear of losing the advertising, called me a scoundrelly demagogue because I told him that his political economy was antiquated and that his biology was contemporaneous with Pliny.

This senator was the tool and the slave, the little puppet of a gross, uneducated machine boss; so was this governor and this supreme court judge; and all three rode on railroad passes. This man, talking soberly and earnestly about the beauties of idealism and the goodness of God, had just betrayed his comrades in a business deal. This man, a pillar of the church and heavy contributor to foreign missions, worked his shop girls ten hours a day on a starvation wage and thereby directly encouraged prostitution. This man, who endowed chairs in universities, perjured himself in courts of law over a matter of dollars and cents.   And this railroad magnate broke his word as a gentleman and a Christian when he granted a secret rebate to one of two captains of industry locked together in a struggle to the death.

It was the same everywhere, crime and betrayal, betrayal and crime—men who were alive, but who were neither clean nor noble, men who were clean and noble but who were not alive.   Then there was a great, hopeless mass, neither noble nor alive, but merely clean.   It did not sin positively nor deliberately; but it did sin passively and ignorantly by acquiescing in the current immorality and profiting by it. Had it been noble and alive it would not have been ignorant, and it would have refused to share in the profits of betrayal and crime.

I discovered that I did not like to live on the parlor floor of society.   Intellectually I was bored.   Morally and spiritually I was sickened.   I remembered my intellectuals and idealists, my unfrocked preachers, broken professors, and clean-minded, class-conscious workingmen.   I remembered my days and nights of sunshine and starshine, where life was all a wild sweet wonder, a spiritual paradise of unselfish adventure and ethical romance.   And I saw before me, ever blazing and burning, the Holy Grail.

So I went back to the working-class, in which I had been born and where I belonged.   I care no longer to climb.   The imposing edifice of society above my head holds no delights for me.   It is the foundation of the edifice that interests me. There I am content to labor, crowbar in hand, shoulder to shoulder with intellectuals, idealists, and class-conscious workingmen, getting a solid pry now and again and setting the whole edifice rocking.   Some day, when we get a few more hands and crowbars to work, we'll topple it over, along with all its rotten life and unburied dead, its monstrous selfishness and sodden materialism.   Then we'll cleanse the cellar and build a new habitation for mankind, in which there will be no parlor floor, in which all the rooms will be bright and airy, and where the air that is breathed will be clean, noble, and alive.

Such is my outlook. I look forward to a time when man shall progress upon something worthier and higher than his stomach, when there will be a finer incentive to impel men to action than the incentive of to-day, which is the incentive of the stomach. I retain my belief in the nobility and excellence of the human. I believe that spiritual sweetness and unselfishness will conquer the gross gluttony of to-day. And last of all, my faith is in the working-class. As some Frenchman has said, "The stairway of time is ever echoing with the wooden shoe going up, the polished boot descending."

November, 1905.

REVOLUTION

REVOLUTION

I RECEIVED a letter the other day. It was from a man in Arizona. It began, "Dear Comrade." It ended, "Yours for the Revolution." I replied to the letter, and my letter began, "Dear Comrade." It ended, "Yours for the Revolution." In the United States there are 400,000 men, of men and women nearly 1,000,000, who begin their letters "Dear Comrade," and end them "Yours for the Revolution." In Germany there are 3,000,000 men who begin their letters "Dear Comrade" and end them "Yours for the Revolution"; in France, 1,000,000 men; in Austria, 800,000 men; in Belgium, 300,000 men; in Italy, 250,000 men; in England, 100,000 men; in Switzerland, 100,000 men; in Denmark, 55,000 men; in Sweden, 50,000 men; in Holland, 40,000 men; in Spain, 30,000 men—comrades all, and revolutionists.

These are numbers which dwarf the grand armies of Napoleon and Xerxes. But they are numbers not of conquest and maintenance of the established order, but of conquest and revolution. They compose, when the roll is called, an army of 7,000,000 men, who, in accordance with the conditions of to-day, are fighting with all their might for the conquest of the wealth of the world and for the complete overthrow of existing society.

There has never been anything like this revolution in the history of the world. There is nothing analogous between it and the American Revolution or the French Revolution. It is unique, colossal. Other revolutions compare with it as asteroids compare with the sun. It is alone of its kind, the first world-revolution in a world whose history is replete with revolutions. And not only this, for it is the first organized movement of men to become a world movement, limited only by the limits of the planet.

This revolution is unlike all other revolutions in many respects. It is not sporadic. It is not a flame of popular discontent, arising in a day and dying down in a day. It is older than the present generation. It has a history and traditions, and a martyr-roll only less extensive possibly than the martyr-roll of Christianity. It has also a literature a myriad times more imposing, scientific, and scholarly than the literature of any previous revolution.

They call themselves "comrades," these men, comrades in the socialist revolution. Nor is the word empty and meaningless, coined of mere lip service. It knits men together as brothers, as men should be knit together who stand shoulder to shoulder under the red banner of revolt. This red banner, by the way, symbolizes the brotherhood of man, and does not symbolize the incendiarism that instantly connects itself with the red banner in the affrighted bourgeois mind. The comradeship of the revolutionists is alive and warm. It passes over geographical lines, transcends race prejudice, and has even proved itself mightier than the Fourth of July, spread-eagle Americanism of our forefathers. The French socialist workingmen and the German socialist workingmen forget Alsace and Lorraine, and, when war threatens, pass resolutions declaring that as workingmen and comrades they have no quarrel with each other. Only the other day, when Japan and Russia sprang at each other's throats, the revolutionists of Japan addressed the following message to the revolutionists of Russia: "Dear Comrades—Your government and ours have recently plunged into war to carry out their imperialistic tendencies, but for us socialists there are no boundaries, race, country, or nationality. We are comrades, brothers and sisters, and have no reason to fight. Your enemies are not the Japanese people, but our militarism and so-called patriotism. Patriotism and militarism are our mutual enemies."

In January, 1905, throughout the United States the socialists held mass-meetings to express their sympathy for their struggling comrades, the revolutionists of Russia, and, more to the point, to furnish the sinews of war by collecting money and cabling it to the Russian leaders.

The fact of this call for money, and the ready response, and the very wording of the call, make a striking and practical demonstration of the international solidarity of this world revolution: "Whatever may be the immediate results of the present revolt in Russia, the socialist propaganda in that country has received from it an impetus unparalleled in the history of modern class wars. The heroic battle for freedom is being fought almost exclusively by the Russian working-class under the intellectual leadership of Russian socialists, thus once more demonstrating the fact that the class-conscious workingmen have become the vanguard of all liberating movements of modern times."

Here are 7,000,000 comrades in an organized, international, world-wide, revolutionary movement. Here is a tremendous human force. It must be reckoned with. Here is power. And here is romance—romance so colossal that it seems to be beyond the ken of ordinary mortals. These revolutionists are swayed by great passion. They have a keen sense of personal right, much of reverence for humanity, but little reverence, if any at all, for the rule of the dead. They refuse to be ruled by the dead. To the bourgeois mind their unbelief in the dominant conventions of the established order is startling. They laugh to scorn the sweet ideals and dear moralities of bourgeois society. They intend to destroy bourgeois society with most of its sweet ideals and dear moralities, and chiefest among these are those that group themselves under such heads as private ownership of capital, survival of the fittest, and patriotism—even patriotism.

Such an army of revolution, 7,000,000 strong, is a thing to make rulers and ruling classes pause and consider. The cry of this army is, "No quarter! We want all that you possess. We will be content with nothing less than all that you possess. We want in our hands the reins of power and the destiny of mankind. Here are our hands. They are strong hands. We are going to take your governments, your palaces, and all your purpled ease away from you, and in that day you shall work for your bread even as the peasant in the field or the starved and runty clerk in your metropolises. Here are our hands. They are strong hands."

Well may rulers and ruling classes pause and consider. This is revolution. And, further, these 7,000,000 men are not an army on paper. Their fighting strength in the field is 7,000,000. To-day they cast 7,000,000 votes in the civilized countries of the world.

Yesterday they were not so strong. To-morrow they will be still stronger. And they are fighters. They love peace. They are unafraid of war. They intend nothing less than to destroy existing capitalist society and to take possession of the whole world. If the law of the land permits, they fight for this end peaceably, at the ballot-box. If the law of the land does not permit, and if they have force meted out to them, they resort to force themselves. They meet violence with violence. Their hands are strong and they are unafraid. In Russia, for instance, there is no suffrage. The government executes the revolutionists. The revolutionists kill the officers of the government. The revolutionists meet legal murder with assassination.

Now here arises a particularly significant phase which would be well for the rulers to consider. Let me make it concrete. I am a revolutionist. Yet I am a fairly sane and normal individual. I speak, and I *think*, of these assassins in Russia as "my comrades." So do all the comrades in America, and all the 7,000,000 comrades in the world. Of what worth an organized, international, revolutionary movement if our comrades are not backed up the world over! The worth is shown by the fact that we do back up the assassinations by our comrades in Russia. They are not disciples of Tolstoy, nor are we. We are revolutionists.

Our comrades in Russia have formed what they call "The Fighting Organization." This Fighting Organization accused, tried, found guilty, and condemned to death, one Sipiaguin,

Minister of Interior.   On April 2 he was shot and killed in
the Maryinsky Palace.   Two years later the Fighting Organization condemned to death and executed another Minister
of Interior, Von Plehve.   Having done so, it issued a document, dated July 29, 1904, setting forth the counts of its
indictment of Von Plehve and its responsibility for the
assassination.   Now, and to the point, this document was
sent out to the socialists of the world, and by them was
published everywhere in the magazines and newspapers.   The
point is, not that the socialists of the world were unafraid
to do it, not that they dared to do it, but that they did it
as a matter of routine, giving publication to what may be
called an official document of the international revolutionary
movement.

These are high lights upon the revolution—granted, but
they are also facts.   And they are given to the rulers and
the ruling classes, not in bravado, not to frighten them, but
for them to consider more deeply the spirit and nature of
this world revolution.   The time has come for the revolution
to demand consideration.   It has fastened upon every civilized
country in the world.   As fast as a country becomes civilized,
the revolution fastens upon it.   With the introduction of
the machine into Japan, socialism was introduced.   Socialism
marched into the Philippines shoulder to shoulder with the
American soldiers.   The echoes of the last gun had scarcely
died away when socialist locals were forming in Cuba and
Porto Rico.   Vastly more significant is the fact that of all
the countries the revolution has fastened upon, on not one
has it relaxed its grip.   On the contrary, on every country its
grip closes tighter year by year.   As an active movement it
began obscurely over a generation ago.   In 1867, its voting
strength in the world was 30,000.   By 1871, its vote had
increased to 100,000.   Not till 1884 did it pass the half-
million point.   By 1889, it had passed the million point.   It
had then gained momentum.   In 1892 the socialist vote of
the world was 1,798,391; in 1893, 2,585,898; in 1895,
3,033,718; in 1898, 4,515,591; in 1902, 5,253,054; in 1903,

6,285,374; and in the year of our Lord 1905 it passed the seven-million mark.

Nor has this flame of revolution left the United States untouched. In 1888, there were only 2,068 socialist votes. In 1902, there were 127,713 socialist votes. And in 1904, 435,040 socialist votes were cast. What fanned this flame? Not hard times. The first four years of the twentieth century were considered prosperous years, yet in that time more than 300,000 men added themselves to the ranks of the revolutionists, flinging their defiance in the teeth of bourgeois society and taking their stand under the blood-red banner. In the state of the writer, California, one man in twelve is an avowed and registered revolutionist.

One thing must be clearly understood. This is no spontaneous and vague uprising of a large mass of discontented and miserable people—a blind and instinctive recoil from hurt. On the contrary, the propaganda is intellectual; the movement is based upon economic necessity and is in line with social evolution; while the miserable people have not yet revolted. The revolutionist is no starved and diseased slave in the shambles at the bottom of the social pit, but is, in the main, a hearty, well-fed workingman, who sees the shambles waiting for him and his children and recoils from the descent. The very miserable people are too helpless to help themselves. But they are being helped, and the day is not far distant when their numbers will go to swell the ranks of the revolutionists.

Another thing must be clearly understood. In spite of the fact that middle-class men and professional men are interested in the movement, it is nevertheless a distinctly working-class revolt. The world over, it is a working-class revolt. The workers of the world, as a class, are fighting the capitalists of the world, as a class. The so-called great middle class is a growing anomaly in the social struggle. It is a perishing class (wily statisticians to the contrary), and its historic mission of buffer between the capitalist- and working-classes has just about been fulfilled. Little remains for it but to wail as it passes into oblivion, as it has already begun to wail in accents Populistic and Jeffersonian-Democratic. The fight is on. The revolution is here now, and it is the world's workers that are in revolt.

Naturally the question arises: Why is this so? No mere whim of the spirit can give rise to a world revolution. Whim does not conduce to unanimity. There must be a deep-seated cause to make 7,000,000 men of the one mind, to make them cast off allegiance to the bourgeois gods and lose faith in so fine a thing as patriotism. There are many counts of the indictment which the revolutionists bring against the capitalist class, but for present use only one need be stated, and it is a count to which capital has never replied and can never reply.

The capitalist class has managed society, and its management has failed. And not only has it failed in its management, but it has failed deplorably, ignobly, horribly. The capitalist class had an opportunity such as was vouchsafed no previous ruling class in the history of the world. It broke away from the rule of the old feudal aristocracy and made modern society. It mastered matter, organized the machinery of life, and made possible a wonderful era for mankind, wherein no creature should cry aloud because it had not enough to eat, and wherein for every child there would be opportunity for education, for intellectual and spiritual uplift. Matter being mastered, and the machinery of life organized, all this was possible. Here was the chance, God-given, and the capitalist class failed. It was blind and greedy. It prattled sweet ideals and dear moralities, rubbed its eyes not once, nor ceased one whit in its greediness, and smashed down in a failure as tremendous only as was the opportunity it had ignored.

But all this is like so much cobwebs to the bourgeois mind. As it was blind in the past, it is blind now and cannot see nor understand. Well, then, let the indictment be stated more definitely, in terms sharp and unmistakable. In the first place, consider the caveman. He was a very simple creature. His head slanted back like an orang-utan's and he had but little more intelligence. He lived in a hostile environment, the prey of all manner of fierce life. He had no inventions nor artifices. His natural efficiency for food-getting was, say, 1. He did not even till the soil. With his natural efficiency of 1, he fought off his carnivorous enemies and got himself food and shelter. He must have done all this, else he would not have multiplied and spread over the earth and sent his progeny down, generation by generation, to become even you and me.

The caveman, with his natural efficiency of 1, got enough to eat most of the time, and no caveman went hungry all the time. Also, he lived a healthy, open-air life, loafed and rested himself, and found plenty of time in which to exercise his imagination and invent gods. That is to say, he did not have to work all his waking moments in order to get enough to eat. The child of the caveman (and this is true of the children of all savage peoples) had a childhood, and by that is meant a happy childhood of play and development.

And now, how fares modern man? Consider the United States, the most prosperous and most enlightened country of the world. In the United States there are 10,000,000 people living in poverty. By poverty is meant that condition of life in which, through lack of food and adequate shelter, the mere standard of working efficiency cannot be maintained. In the United States there are 10,000,000 people who have not enough to eat. In the United States, because they have not enough to eat, there are 10,000,000 people who cannot keep the ordinary measure of strength in their bodies. This means that these 10,000,000 people are perishing, are dying, body and soul, slowly, because they have not enough to eat. All over this broad, prosperous, enlightened land, are men, women, and children who are living miserably. In all the great cities, where they are segregated in slum ghettos by hundreds of thousands and by millions, their misery becomes beastliness. No caveman ever starved as chronically as they starve, ever slept as vilely as they sleep, ever festered with rottenness and disease as they fester, nor ever toiled as hard and for as long hours as they toil.

In Chicago there is a woman who toiled sixty hours per week. She was a garment worker. She sewed buttons on clothes. Among the Italian garment workers of Chicago, the average weekly wage of the dressmakers is 90 cents, but they work every week in the year. The average weekly wage of the pants finishers is $1.31, and the average number of weeks employed in the year is 27.85. The average yearly earnings of the dressmakers is $47.00; of the pants finishers, $37.00. Such wages means no childhood for the children, beastliness of living, and starvation for all.

Unlike the caveman, modern man cannot get food and shelter whenever he feels like working for it. Modern man has first to find the work, and in this he is often unsuccessful. Then misery becomes acute. This acute misery is chronicled daily in the newspapers. Let several of the countless instances be cited.

In New York City lived a woman, Mary Mead. She had three children: Mary, one year old; Johanna, two years old; Alice, four years old. Her husband could find no work. They starved. They were evicted from their shelter at 160 Steuben Street. Mary Mead strangled her baby, Mary, one year old; strangled Alice, four years old; failed to strangle Johanna, two years old, and then herself took poison. Said the father to the police: "Constant poverty had driven my wife insane. We lived at No. 160 Steuben Street until a week ago, when we were dispossessed. I could get no work. I could not even make enough to put food into our mouths. The babies grew ill and weak. My wife cried nearly all the time."

"So overwhelmed is the Department of Charities with tens of thousands of applications from men out of work that it finds itself unable to cope with the situation."—*New York Commercial*, January 11, 1905.

In a daily paper, because he cannot get work in order to get something to eat, modern man advertises as follows:—

"Young man, good education, unable to obtain employment, will sell to physician and bacteriologist for experimental purposes all right and title to his body. Address for price, box 3466, *Examiner*."

"Frank A. Mallin went to the central police station Wednesday night and asked to be locked up on a charge of vagrancy. He said he had been conducting an unsuccessful search for work so long that he was sure he must be a vagrant. In any event, he was so hungry he must be fed. Police Judge Graham sentenced him to ninety days' imprisonment."— *San Francisco Examiner*.

In a room at the Soto House, 32 Fourth Street, San Francisco, was found the body of W. G. Robbins. He had turned on the gas. Also was found his diary, from which the following extracts are made:—

"March 3.—No chance of getting anything here. What will I do?

"March 7.—Cannot find anything yet.

"March 8.—Am living on doughnuts at five cents a day.

"March 9.—My last quarter gone for room rent.

"March 10.—God help me. Have only five cents left. Can get nothing to do. What next? Starvation or—? I have spent my last nickel to-night. What shall I do? Shall it be steal, beg, or die? I have never stolen, begged, or starved in all my fifty years of life, but now I am on the brink—death seems the only refuge.

"March 11.—Sick all day—burning fever this afternoon. Had nothing to eat to-day or since yesterday noon. My head, my head. Good-by, all."

How fares the child of modern man in this most prosperous of lands? In the city of New York 50,000 children go hungry to school every morning. From the same city on January 12, a press despatch was sent out over the country of a case reported by Dr. A. E. Daniel, of the New York Infirmary for Women and Children. The case was that of a babe, eighteen months old, who earned by its labor fifty cents per week in a tenement sweat-shop.

"On a pile of rags in a room bare of furniture and freezing cold, Mrs. Mary Gallin, dead from starvation, with an emaciated baby four months old crying at her breast, was found this morning at 513 Myrtle Avenue, Brooklyn, by Policeman McConnon of the Flushing Avenue Station. Huddled together for warmth in another part of the room were the father, James Gallin, and three children ranging from two to eight years of age. The children gazed at the policeman much as ravenous animals might have done. They were famished, and there was not a vestige of food in their comfortless home."—*New York Journal*, January 2, 1902.

In the United States 80,000 children are toiling out their lives in the textile mills alone. In the South they work twelve-hour shifts. They never see the day. Those on the night shift are asleep when the sun pours its life and warmth over the world, while those on the day shift are at the machines before dawn and return to their miserable dens, called "homes," after dark. Many receive no more than ten cents a day. There are babies who work for five and six cents a day. Those who work on the night shift are often kept awake by having cold water dashed in their faces. There are children six years of age who have already to their credit eleven months' work on the night shift. When they become sick, and are unable to rise from their beds to go to work, there are men employed to go on horseback from house to house, and cajole and bully them into arising and going to work. Ten per cent of them contract active consumption. All are puny wrecks, distorted, stunted, mind and body. Elbert Hubbard says of the child-laborers of the Southern cotton-mills:—

"I thought to lift one of the little toilers to ascertain his weight. Straightaway through his thirty-five pounds of skin and bones there ran a tremor of fear, and he struggled forward to tie a broken thread. I attracted his attention by a touch, and offered him a silver dime. He looked at me dumbly from a face that might have belonged to a man of sixty, so furrowed, tightly drawn, and full of pain it was. He did not reach for the money—he did not know what it was. There were dozens of such children in this particular mill.

A physician who was with me said that they would all be dead probably in two years, and their places filled by others —there were plenty more. Pneumonia carries off most of them. Their systems are ripe for disease, and when it comes there is no rebound—no response. Medicine simply does not act—nature is whipped, beaten, discouraged, and the child sinks into a stupor and dies."

So fares modern man and the child of modern man in the United States, most prosperous and enlightened of all countries on earth. It must be remembered that the instances given are instances only, but that they can be multiplied myriads of times. It must also be remembered that what is true of the United States is true of all the civilized world. Such misery was not true of the caveman. Then what has happened? Has the hostile environment of the caveman grown more hostile for his descendants? Has the caveman's natural efficiency of 1 for food-getting and shelter-getting diminished in modern man to one-half or one-quarter?

On the contrary, the hostile environment of the caveman has been destroyed. For modern man it no longer exists. All carnivorous enemies, the daily menace of the younger world, have been killed off. Many of the species of prey have become extinct. Here and there, in secluded portions of the world, still linger a few of man's fiercer enemies. But they are far from being a menace to mankind. Modern man, when he wants recreation and change, goes to the secluded portions of the world for a hunt. Also, in idle moments, he wails regretfully at the passing of the "big game," which he knows in the not distant future will disappear from the earth.

Nor since the day of the caveman has man's efficiency for food-getting and shelter-getting diminished. It has increased a thousand-fold. Since the day of the caveman, matter has been mastered. The secrets of matter have been discovered. Its laws have been formulated. Wonderful artifices have been made, and marvellous inventions, all tending to increase tremendously man's natural efficiency of 1 in every food-

getting, shelter-getting exertion, in farming, mining, manu-
facturing, transportation, and communication.

From the caveman to the hand-workers of three generations
ago, the increase in efficiency for food- and shelter-getting
has been very great. But in this day, by machinery, the
efficiency of the hand-worker of three generations ago has in
turn been increased many times. Formerly it required 200
hours of human labor to place 100 tons of ore on a railroad
car. To-day, aided by machinery, but two hours of human
labor is required to do the same task. The United States
Bureau of Labor is responsible for the following table, showing
the comparatively recent increase in man's food- and shelter-
getting efficiency:

	Machine Hours.	Hand Hours.
Barley (100 bushels)	9	211
Corn (50 bushels shelled, stalks, husks, and blades cut into fodder)	34	228
Oats (160 bushels)	28	265
Wheat (50 bushels)	7	160
Loading ore (loading 100 tons iron ore on cars) . .	2	200
Unloading coal (transferring 200 tons from canal-boats to bins 400 feet distant)	20	240
Pitchforks (50 pitchforks, 12-inch tines)	12	200
Plough (one landside plough, oak beams and handles)	3	118

According to the same authority, under the best conditions
for organization in farming, labor can produce 20 bushels of
wheat for 66 cents, or 1 bushel for 3 1/3 cents. This was
done on a bonanza farm of 10,000 acres in California, and
was the average cost of the whole product of the farm. Mr.
Carroll D. Wright says that to-day 4,500,000 men, aided by
machinery, turn out a product that would require the labor
of 40,000,000 men if produced by hand. Professor Herzog,
of Austria, says that 5,000,000 people with the machinery of
to-day, employed at socially useful labor, would be able to
supply a population of 20,000,000 people with all the neces-

saries and small luxuries of life by working 1½ hours per day.

This being so, matter being mastered, man's efficiency for food- and shelter-getting being increased a thousand-fold over the efficiency of the caveman, then why is it that millions of modern men live more miserably than lived the caveman? This is the question the revolutionist asks, and he asks it of the managing class, the capitalist class. The capitalist class does not answer it. The capitalist class cannot answer it.

If modern man's food- and shelter-getting efficiency is a thousand-fold greater than that of the caveman, why, then, are there 10,000,000 people in the United States to-day who are not properly sheltered and properly fed? If the child of the caveman did not have to work, why, then, to-day, in the United States, are 80,000 children working out their lives in the textile factories alone? If the child of the caveman did not have to work, why, then, to-day, in the United States, are there 1,752,187 child-laborers?

It is a true count in the indictment. The capitalist class has mismanaged, is to-day mismanaging. In New York City 50,000 children go hungry to school, and in New York City there are 1320 millionaires. The point, however, is not that the mass of mankind is miserable because of the wealth the capitalist class has taken to itself. Far from it. The point really is that the mass of mankind is miserable, not for want of the wealth taken by the capitalist class, *but for want of the wealth that was never created*. This wealth was never created because the capitalist class managed too wastefully and irrationally. The capitalist class, blind and greedy, grasping madly, has not only not made the best of its management, but made the worst of it. It is a management prodigiously wasteful. This point cannot be emphasized too strongly.

In face of the facts that modern man lives more wretchedly than the caveman, and that modern man's food- and shelter-getting efficiency is a thousand-fold greater than the caveman's, no other solution is possible than that the management is prodigiously wasteful.

With the natural resources of the world, the machinery already invented, a rational organization of production and distribution, and an equally rational elimination of waste, the able-bodied workers would not have to labor more than two or three hours per day to feed everybody, clothe everybody, house everybody, educate everybody, and give a fair measure of little luxuries to everybody. There would be no more material want and wretchedness, no more children toiling out their lives, no more men and women and babes living like beasts and dying like beasts. Not only would matter be mastered, but the machine would be mastered. In such a day incentive would be finer and nobler than the incentive of to-day, which is the incentive of the stomach. No man, woman, or child would be impelled to action by an empty stomach. On the contrary, they would be impelled to action as a child in a spelling match is impelled to action, as boys and girls at games, as scientists formulating law, as inventors applying law, as artists and sculptors painting canvases and shaping clay, as poets and statesmen serving humanity by singing and by statecraft. The spiritual, intellectual, and artistic uplift consequent upon such a condition of society would be tremendous. All the human world would surge upward in a mighty wave.

This was the opportunity vouchsafed the capitalist class. Less blindness on its part, less greediness, and a rational management, were all that was necessary. A wonderful era was possible for the human race. But the capitalist class failed. It made a shambles of civilization. Nor can the capitalist class plead not guilty. It knew of the opportunity. Its wise men told it of the opportunity, its scholars and its scientists told it of the opportunity. All that they said is there to-day in the books, just so much damning evidence against it. It would not listen. It was too greedy. It rose up (as it rises up to-day), shamelessly, in our legislative halls, and declared that profits were impossible without the toil of children and babes. It lulled its conscience to sleep with prattle of sweet ideals and dear moralities, and allowed the suffering and misery of mankind to continue and to increase. In short, the capitalist class failed to take advantage of the opportunity.

But the opportunity is still here. The capitalist class has been tried and found wanting. Remains the working-class to see what it can do with the opportunity. "But the working-class is incapable," says the capitalist class. "What do you know about it?" the working-class replies. "Because you have failed is no reason that we shall fail. Furthermore, we are going to have a try at it, anyway. Seven millions of us say so. And what have you to say to that?"

And what can the capitalist class say? Grant the incapacity of the working-class. Grant that the indictment and the argument of the revolutionists are all wrong. The 7,000,000 revolutionists remain. Their existence is a fact. Their belief in their capacity, and in their indictment and their argument, is a fact. Their constant growth is a fact. Their intention to destroy present-day society is a fact, as is also their intention to take possession of the world with all its wealth and machinery and governments. Moreover, it is a fact that the working-class is vastly larger than the capitalist class.

The revolution is a revolution of the working-class. How can the capitalist class, in the minority, stem this tide of revolution? What has it to offer? What does it offer? Employers' associations, injunctions, civil suits for plundering of the treasuries of the labor-unions, clamor and combination for the open shop, bitter and shameless opposition to the eight-hour day, strong efforts to defeat all reform child-labor bills, graft in every municipal council, strong lobbies and bribery in every legislature for the purchase of capitalist legislation, bayonets, machine-guns, policemen's clubs, professional strike-breakers, and armed Pinkertons—these are the things the capitalist class is dumping in front of the tide of revolution, as though, forsooth, to hold it back.

The capitalist class is as blind to-day to the menace of the revolution as it was blind in the past to its own God-given opportunity. It cannot see how precarious is its position, cannot comprehend the power and the portent of the revolution. It goes on its placid way, prattling sweet ideals and dear moralities, and scrambling sordidly for material benefits.

No overthrown ruler or class in the past ever considered the revolution that overthrew it, and so with the capitalist class of to-day. Instead of compromising, instead of lengthening its lease of life by conciliation and by removal of some of the harsher oppressions of the working-class, it antagonizes the working-class, drives the working class into revolution. Every broken strike in recent years, every legally plundered trades-union treasury, every closed shop made into an open shop, has driven the members of the working-class directly hurt over to socialism by hundreds and thousands. Show a workingman that his union fails, and he becomes a revolutionist. Break a strike with an injunction or bankrupt a union with a civil suit, and the workingmen hurt thereby listen to the siren song of the socialist and are lost forever to the *political capitalist* parties.

Antagonism never lulled revolution, and antagonism is about all the capitalist class offers. It is true, it offers some few antiquated notions which were very efficacious in the past, but which are no longer efficacious. Fourth-of-July liberty in terms of the Declaration of Independence and of the French Encyclopedists is scarcely apposite to-day. It does not appeal to the workingman who has had his head broken by a policeman's club, his union treasury bankrupted by a court decision, or his job taken away from him by a labor-saving invention. Nor does the Constitution of the United States appear so glorious and constitutional to the workingman who has experienced a bull pen or been unconstitutionally deported from Colorado. Nor are this particular workingman's hurt feelings soothed by reading in the newspapers that both the bull pen and the deportation were preëminently just, legal, and constitutional. "To hell, then, with the Constitution!" says he, and another revolutionist has been made—by the capitalist class.

In short, so blind is the capitalist class that it does nothing to lengthen its lease of life, while it does everything to shorten it. The capitalist class offers nothing that is clean, noble, and alive. The revolutionists offer everything that is clean, noble, and alive. They offer service, unselfishness, sacrifice, martyrdom—the things that sting awake the imagination of the people, touching their hearts with the fervor that arises out of the impulse toward good and which is essentially religious in its nature.

But the revolutionists blow hot and blow cold. They offer facts and statistics, economics and scientific arguments. If the workingman be merely selfish, the revolutionists show him, mathematically demonstrate to him, that his condition will be bettered by the revolution. If the workingman be the higher type, moved by impulses toward right conduct, if he have soul and spirit, the revolutionists offer him the things of the soul and the spirit, the tremendous things that cannot be measured by dollars and cents, nor be held down by dollars and cents. The revolutionist cries out upon wrong and injustice, and preaches righteousness. And, most potent of all, he sings the eternal song of human freedom—a song of all lands and all tongues and all time.

Few members of the capitalist class see the revolution. Most of them are too ignorant, and many are too afraid to see it. It is the same old story of every perishing ruling class in the world's history. Fat with power and possession, drunken with success, and made soft by surfeit and by cessation of struggle, they are like the drones clustered about the honey vats when the worker-bees spring upon them to end their rotund existence.

President Roosevelt vaguely sees the revolution, is frightened by it, and recoils from seeing it. As he says: "Above all, we need to remember that any kind of class animosity in the political world is, if possible, even more wicked, even more destructive to national welfare, than sectional, race, or religious animosity."

Class animosity in the political world, President Roosevelt maintains, is wicked. But class animosity in the political world is the preachment of the revolutionists. "Let the class wars in the industrial world continue," they say, "but extend the class war to the political world." As their leader, Eugene V. Debs, says: "So far as this struggle is concerned, there is no good capitalist and no bad workingman. Every capitalist is your enemy and every workingman is your friend."

Here is class animosity in the political world with a vengeance. And here is revolution. In 1888 there were only 2,000 revolutionists of this type in the United States; in 1900 there were 127,000 revolutionists; in 1904, 435,000 revolutionists. Wickedness of the President Roosevelt definition evidently flourishes and increases in the United States. Quite so, for it is the revolution that flourishes and increases.

Here and there a member of the capitalist class catches a clear glimpse of the revolution, and raises a warning cry. But his class does not heed. President Eliot of Harvard raised such a cry: "I am forced to believe there is a present danger of socialism never before so imminent in America in so dangerous a form, because never before imminent in so well organized a form. The danger lies in the obtaining control of the trades-unions by the socialists." And the capitalist employers, instead of giving heed to the warnings, are perfecting their strike-breaking organization and combining more strongly than ever for a general assault upon that dearest of all things to the trades-unions,—the closed shop. In so far as this assault succeeds, by just that much will the capitalist class shorten its lease of life. It is the old, old story, over again and over again. The drunken drones still cluster greedily about the honey vats.

Possibly one of the most amusing spectacles of to-day is the attitude of the American press toward the revolution. It is also a pathetic spectacle. It compels the onlooker to be aware of a distinct loss of pride in his species. Dogmatic utterance from the mouth of ignorance may make gods laugh, but it should make men weep. And the American editors (in the general instance) are so impressive about it! The old "divide-up," "men-are-*not*-born-free-and-equal" propositions are enunciated gravely and sagely, as things white-hot and new from the forge of human wisdom. Their feeble vaporings show no more than a schoolboy's comprehension of the nature of the revolution. Parasites themselves on the capitalist class, serving the capitalist class by moulding public opinion, they, too, cluster drunkenly about the honey vats.

Of course, this is true only of the large majority of American editors. To say that it is true of all of them would be to cast too great obloquy upon the human race. Also, it would be untrue, for here and there an occasional editor does see clearly—and in his case, ruled by stomach-incentive, is usually afraid to say what he thinks about it. So far as the science and the sociology of the revolution are concerned, the average editor is a generation or so behind the facts. He is intellectually slothful, accepts no facts until they are accepted by the majority, and prides himself upon his conservatism. He is an instinctive optimist, prone to believe that what ought to be, is. The revolutionist gave this up long ago, and believes not that what ought to be, is, but what is, is, and that it may not be what it ought to be at all.

Now and then, rubbing his eyes vigorously, an editor catches a sudden glimpse of the revolution and breaks out in naïve volubility, as, for instance, the one who wrote the following in the *Chicago Chronicle*: "American socialists are revolutionists. They know that they are revolutionists. It is high time that other people should appreciate the fact." A white-hot, brand-new discovery, and he proceeded to shout it out from the housetops that we, forsooth, were revolutionists. Why, it is just what we have been doing all these years—shouting it out from the housetops that we are revolutionists, and stop us who can.

The time should be past for the mental attitude: "Revolution is atrocious. Sir, there is no revolution." Likewise should the time be past for that other familiar attitude: "Socialism is slavery. Sir, it will never be." It is no longer a question of dialectics, theories, and dreams. There is no question about it. The revolution is a fact. It is here now. Seven million revolutionists, organized, working day and night, are preaching the revolution—that passionate gospel, the Brotherhood of Man. Not only is it a cold-blooded economic propaganda, but it is in essence a religious propaganda with a fervor in it of Paul and Christ. The capitalist class has been indicted. It has failed in its management and its management is to be taken away from it. Seven million men of the working-class say that they are going to get the rest of the working-class to join with them and take the management away. The revolution is here, now. Stop it who can.

March, 1905.

Hardbacks

Author - Jack London

$34.75.............ESSAYS OF REVOLT (original cover)

$43.75.............MARTIN EDEN

$36.75.............WAR OF THE CLASSES

$36.75.............JOHN BARLEYCORN

$33.75.............THE PEOPLE OF THE ABYSS

$34.75.............JACK LONDON ON THE ROAD

$35.75.............THE ASSASSINATION BUREAU, LTD.

$36.75.............THE IRON HEEL

Author – Bruno Traven

$32.75.............GENERAL FROM THE JUNGLE

$38.75.............THE DEATH SHIP

$35.75.............THE REBELLION OF THE HANGED

$34.75.............THE WHITE ROSE

$34.75.............THE BRIDGE IN THE JUNGLE

$34.75..............MARCH TO THE MONTERIA

$37.95..............THE TREASURE OF THE SIERRA MADRE

Author – Carl Frederick

$39.95................est: PLAYING THE GAME THE NEW WAY

Author – Mao Tsetung

$39.75.................QUOTATIONS FROM CHAIRMAN MAO TSETUNG (original cover)

Author – Upton Sinclair

$33.75.................OUR LADY

$44.75.................OIL (original cover)

$39.75.................THE JUNGLE (original cover)

$32.75.................THE FLIVVER KING: THE STORY OF FORD-AMERICA

$35.75.................ONE HUNDRED PERCENT: THE STORY OF A PATRIOT

$37,75.................WORLD'S END I

$42.75.................WORLD'S END II

$34.75.................THE SECRET LIFE OF JESUS

$34.75.................THE MONEYCHANGERS

$35.75.................MENTAL RADIO

$35.75.................THE MILLENIUM

$35.75.................A PERSONAL JESUS

$36.75.................PROFITS OF RELIGION

$34.95................THEY CALL ME CARPENTER: A TALE OF THE SECOND COMING

$45.75..................DRAGON'S TEETH
(1943 Pulitzer Prize Winner)(original cover)

Author – Thomas Paine

$38.75................COMMON SENSE & THE RIGHTS OF MAN & THE AGE OF REASON

$33.75................THE AMERICAN CRISIS

Author – Karl Marx

$39.75................DAS KAPITAL

$33.75................THE COMMUNIST MANIFESTO & WAGES, PRICE AND PROFIT

$32.75................WAGE-LABOUR AND CAPITAL & VALUE, PRICE AND PROFIT

Author – W. E. B. Du Bois

$34.75................THE SOULS OF BLACK FOLK

Author – Eugene Debs

$35.75................WALLS AND BARS

Author – Jean-Jacques Rousseau

$34.75................THE SOCIAL CONTRACT

Author – John Reed

$37.75................TEN DAYS THAT SHOOK THE WORLD

$36.75................INSURGENT MEXICO

Author – Antonio Gramsci

$33.75................THE MODERN PRINCE AND SELECTED
WRITINGS

Author – V. I. Lenin

$35.75................THE STATE AND REVOLUTION

$36.95................FIGHT AGAINST STALINISM &
IMPERIALISM: THE HIGHEST STAGE OF
CAPITALISM

Author – John Dewey

$35.75................HOW WE THINK & EDUCATION
AND EXPERIENCE

$37.75................INDIVIDUALISM OLD AND NEW &
LIBERALISM AND SOCIAL ACTION & A COMMON FAITH

$39.75................DEMOCRACY AND EDUCATION &
FREEDOM AND CULTURE

Author – David Ricardo

$37.75................PRINCIPLES OF POLITICAL ECONOMY
AND TAXATION

Author – Thomas Jefferson

$34.75................BIOGRAPHY OF THOMAS JEFFERSON &
THE LIFE AND MORALS OF JESUS OF NAZARETH

Author – Emma Goldman

$35.95................ANARCHISM AND OTHER WRITINGS

Author – Rosa Luxemburg

$32.95................REFORM OR REVOLUTION &
THE MASS STRIKE

Author – Leon Trotsky

$35.75................THE REVOLUTION BETRAYED

Author – John Stuart Mill

$33.95................ON SOCIALISM & THE SUBJECTION
OF WOMEN

Author – Friedrich Nietzsche

$34.75................BEYOND GOOD AND EVIL

$40.75..................THE BIRTH OF TRAGEDY &
75 APHORISMS & THE ANTI-CHRIST

Author – John Quincy Adams

$33.95..................THE AMISTAD ARGUMENT &
THE STATE OF THE UNION ADDRESSES

Author's – James Madison. Alexander Hamilton
and John Jay

$40.75..................THE FEDERALIST PAPERS

Author – G .W. Friedrich Hegel

$43.75..................THE PHILOSOPHY OF HISTORY

Softcovers

Author – Bruno Traven

$22.95.....................THE DEATH SHIP

Author – Jack London

$21.95.....................JACK LONDON ON THE ROAD

$14.95.....................THE PEOPLE OF THE ABYSS

$16.95.....................THE ASSASSINATION BUREAU, LTD.

$18.95.....................THE IRON HEEL

$17.95.....................JOHN BARLEYCORN

$24.95.....................MARTIN EDEN

Author – Frederick Ellis & Carl Frederick

$19.95......................THE OAKLAND STATEMENT

(original cover)